Learning Counseling and Problem-Solving Skills

ABOUT THE AUTHORS

LESLIE E. BORCK, Ph.D., Director of the Westchester County, New York, Self-Help Clearinghouse, is a psychologist at Harlem Valley Psychiatric Center as well as in private practice. Dr. Borck has authored numerous articles and presentations on such topics as the training of nonprofessional counselors, communication and job-finding skills, self-help, and mutual aid. She has developed counseling and communications training programs for Veterans Administration personnel, students, and nonprofessional community helpers.

STEPHEN B. FAWCETT, Ph.D., is Associate Professor, Department of Human Development and Family Life, and Research Associate and Coordinator of the Community Development program for the Center for Public Affairs at the University of Kansas. Dr. Fawcett has authored numerous articles on such topics as personalized instruction, community education, nonprofessional training, and community application of instructional technology. In addition, he has developed a variety of training programs for students ranging in educational background from high school dropout to graduate level. Dr. Fawcett has served as consulting editor for a number of journals including the *American Journal of Community Psychology*, the *Journal of Social Welfare*, *Behavioral Assessment* and *Behavior Therapy*. He is currently on the editorial boards of *ETC (Education and Training of Children)* and the *Journal of Applied Behavior Analysis*.

Learning Counseling and Problem-Solving Skills

Leslie E. Borck, Ph.D.
Stephen B. Fawcett, Ph.D.

The Haworth Press
New York

The Haworth Press, Inc.
28 East 22 Street
New York, NY 10010

Edited and designed by Trudy Raschkind Steinfeld. Cold type composition for Parts I and II by Bettyanne Palmer of Strong Silent Type, Florida, N.Y. Typewriter composition for Part III by Liz McGehee, New York, N.Y.

Library of Congress Cataloging in Publication Data

Borck, Leslie E.
   Learning counseling and problem-solving skills.

   Includes index.
   1. Counseling—Programmed instruction. 2. Problem solving—Programmed instruction. I. Fawcett, Stephen B. II. Title.
BF637.C6B59   158'.3   82—2916
ISBN 0—917724—30—5   AACR2
ISBN 0—917724—35—6 (pbk.)

Printed in the United States of America

For my mother and father, Jackie, Doug,
Devananda, and dear friends, all of whom
have graced my life with their love.
L.E.B.

For Cindy Jo, Katie, John, Tommy,
my Dad, my brother, and all those
whose eyes tell us that we have worth.
S.B.F.

Contents

Preface

Philosopher Mortimer Adler, editor of an acclaimed edition of the Encyclopedia Britannica, likes to talk about giving away knowledge—putting it in a form that others can absorb. Our aim is similar: to capture some of the magic of the skilled helper and to communicate it so that others may share in the benefits of these skills. We have reviewed our own counseling and problem-solving experiences, sought the advice of others, and read much of what is written on the art of helping. The helping skills identified in this search were then elaborated in a series of lessons using experimentally tested teaching methods. These lessons were carefully evaluated, and the revised versions appear in this book. Thus, *Learning Counseling and Problem-Solving Skills* and the accompanying *Instructor's Manual* are the results of these efforts in developing a rapid and effective method of teaching the skills of helping.

Helping skills have general applicability to a variety of situations at work or with your family, friends, or neighbors. Drawing on an array of everyday counseling situations, this book is appropriate for students interested in such professions as counseling, psychology, social welfare, medicine, public administration, personnel management, and other areas of social service employment. In addition, the book's emphasis on problem solving makes it particularly well suited to the needs of volunteers and nonprofessionals in such settings as community service agencies, halfway houses; group homes, telephone hot lines, crisis information centers, self-help groups, and other United Way agencies.

This book weds the skills of counseling and problem solving as they might be used in everyday situations. Using a combination of reading assignments, exercises, and practice, the book includes the counseling skills necessary for developing a good client-helper relationship. Students will also read about and practice the problem-solving skills that help clients or neighbors clarify their problems, identify ways to improve the situations, and make decisions about what to do. As such, this text is appropriate for college and university courses, independent study, workshops, and inservice training.

Writing a book is a bit like baking bread. We have assembled the ingredients, kneaded the dough, and let it rise. But though the method is familiar, the ingredients for this recipe are unique:

ADD: one heaping dose of feedback on the completeness of the training method from experienced counselors. We are especially grateful to Jim Lichtenberg, Dick Rundquist, and Art Thomas in this regard.

ADD: experience from the grassroots community service workers on the kinds of problems from which people suffer, possible alternative solutions, and the likely consequences of such alternatives. We are particularly indebted to Ocoee Miller for her substantial contribution to the Problem-Solving Index.

MIX THOROUGHLY: and give the manuscript to a good teacher and interested students for field-testing. Special thanks to Paula Whang for the many improvements lent by her thoughtful teaching approach. Thanks also to Kay Fletcher, Mark Mathews, Holly Hale, and Mike Everhart for their many helpful suggestions.

ADD: inspiration for the project and a testing ground for its utility. We will always be grateful to the low-income families who make up the Penn House community service center in Lawrence, Kansas, and to Barbara Thompson and Bessie Nichols in particular, for encouraging us to develop this training program.

BAKE

AND LET COOL: and give the completed work to an excellent editor for her finecombing and improvements. Our most sincere thanks to Trudy Raschkind Steinfeld for her assistance.

This book would not have been possible without the hospitality of the Center for Public Affairs at the University of Kansas.

Learning Counseling and Problem-Solving Skills

PART I
INTRODUCTION

1

Toward the
Skilled Helper

Give a man a fish, and you feed him for a day.
Teach a man to fish, and you feed him for a lifetime.

—*Chinese proverb*

To act for persons in distress is to provide temporary help; to help them help themselves is to provide true assistance. The skilled helper listens to problems and helps clarify potential solutions. He or she opens up options for the client, helping identify alternatives for solving problems. In skilled helping, the client coproduces alternatives and helps analyze the most appropriate option. Accordingly, the skilled helper does not solve problems *for* clients, but *leads* them in finding their own solutions.

Our assistance is needed by those around us, whether we are professional or nonprofessional helpers, whether our services are free or for a fee. The husband, wife, single parent, teenager, or retired person who asks for help with a problem does not demand to see our training credentials before describing his or her concerns. Each of us, regardless of schooling or experience, listens to the problems of others and helps as well as possible.

This book is predicated on two rather simple premises. First, there are many talented helpers out there who have much to offer those who seek their assistance. Each of us has something to bring to another person, whether we are mental health workers, counselors, social workers, psychologists, police, nonprofessional service workers, crisis center volunteers, or good neighbors. Each of us has unique helping strengths such as warmth, sensitivity, genuine caring, or common sense. Such personal strengths are foundations on which positive helping is based.

It is also assumed that our helping efforts might be more effective if based on carefully evaluated counseling and problem-solving methods. Some ways of interacting with clients and analyzing their problems appear to be more effective than others. For example, such skills as listening actively, asking questions, reflecting feelings, summarizing, and solving problems may improve relationships with clients and the chances of helping with their problems. Such fundamental counseling and problem-solving skills are the objectives of this skill training program.

2

The Training Method and Its Evaluation

An array of training methods is available with the goal of teaching various helping skills. This book, like the others, is designed to teach relevant helping methods. However, our book differs from many related texts in several important ways.

First, this text brings together the basic skills of counseling *and* problem solving. The skills of a good helper—listening actively, reflecting feelings, asking questions, summarizing, and opening and closing helping sessions—are central to competent helping. However, insofar as helpers are asked to do more than just listen—and are asked actually to help clients solve real problems—other skills are also needed. Problem-solving skills include helping clients to clarify their problem situations, to identify alternatives available to change the situation, to consider the consequences of the alternatives, and to begin to make decisions about what to do. In combination, these counseling and problem-solving skills represent a strong basis for positive helping.

Second, experimentally tested methods of behavioral instruction are used to teach these counseling and problem-solving skills. Years of research and development have shown that examples, study guides, practice, and feedback are particularly effective in teaching new skills. These behavioral teaching methods have been combined in a series of training lessons for each of the major skills of counseling and problem solving.

Third, the training lessons used in this book were carefully evaluated in formal research studies. In one study, we evaluated the effectiveness of the training lessons in teaching counseling and problem-solving skills to university students (Borck, Fawcett, & Lichtenberg, 1979). We found that the counseling and problem-solving skills identified in this text rose to nearly perfect levels following the reading, practice, and feedback outlined in this book. In addition, expert ratings showed an increase in the quality of counseling performance and in students' confidence in their helping abilities. Students were highly satisfied with the training method and the new skills that they had learned (Borck, Fawcett, & Lichtenberg, in press). In a second study, we found similar effects with nonprofessional social service workers, who also mastered the skills, gained in self-confidence, and reported satisfaction with the text (Whang, Fletcher, & Fawcett, in press). Thus, effectiveness of this text has been documented in formal research studies.

These three factors—the learning of both counseling and problem-solving skills, the use of experimentally tested methods of instruction, and the careful evaluation of these training lessons—contribute to the uniqueness of this text.

HOW WAS THE METHOD DEVELOPED?

The counseling and problem-solving skills that you will be learning were identified in a review of the literature, an examination of many related training programs, and conversations with professional counselors. In addition, we spent many hours studying good and bad examples of counseling and problem solving in hopes of identifying the most important helping skills. These skills were then broken down into their many parts so that they might be learned more easily. Finally, drawing from our own experience in helping people with problems and teaching these skills to others, we prepared, field tested, and revised each of the training lessons. The training lessons are the result of these research and development efforts.

WHAT IS THE TRAINING METHOD?

The training lessons contain descriptions of the when, why, and how of each counseling and problem-solving skill. These detailed instructions are followed by study guide questions by which the student may test his or her knowledge of the information. The student is given a chance to practice the skills in role-playing situations; feedback is provided by the instructor or a student partner. Thus, the training method combines instructions, examples, rationales, study guides, practice, and feedback in a highly effective teaching format.

So, you may expect that your time with this book will be rewarded with new skills of helping and increased confidence in your abilities to counsel people with problems. The efficiency of this learning method makes it a practical approach to learning skills for helping others.

REFERENCES

Borck, L. E., Fawcett, S. B., and Lichtenberg, J. W. Training counseling and problem-solving skills with university students. *American Journal of Community Psychology* (in press).
Whang, P. L., Fletcher, R. K., and Fawcett, S. B. Training counseling skills: An experimental analysis and social validation. *Journal of Applied Behavior Analysis* (in press).

3

Introduction for the Student

Helpers are in a very responsible position. People come to them for assistance of all kinds. It can be very difficult asking for help. Anyone trusting you with his or her personal feelings and thoughts deserves your best efforts. Good helpers are effective users of every counseling and problem-solving skill in this book. Thus, it is important for you to take time to master each skill.

These training lessons are for those who want to learn how to communicate more effectively. Helping skills are really just good communication skills. To help others form a trusting relationship, to help them talk about what's on their minds, or to help them make decisions—that is what good counseling and problem-solving are all about.

Helping skills, like any new skills, take practice before they seem natural. You may initially find that these skills feel phony and unnatural. However, once they do become natural and part of your normal communication style, you may find that you have improved your abilities to communicate with family, friends, teachers, and employers. You should be able to listen more closely, be more sensitive to people's feelings, and know what to say to communicate more effectively. Such skills should be of great assistance in your future helping relationships.

ARE YOU WELL SUITED TO THE COUNSELING ROLE?

Effective helpers seem to have certain qualities. Some might describe these persons as "warm," "trustworthy," "interested," "genuine," or maybe even just "nice." If you are motivated you, too, can learn the skills of interacting more effectively with other people.

Good helpers care! If you like people, enjoy talking to people (but, more important, like listening to people), respect the other's privacy, and are willing to help solve someone's problem without putting him or her down for being in trouble, you may be well suited to the counseling role.

WHAT CAN YOU EXPECT FROM THIS TRAINING?

Skilled helpers are involved in counseling people with problems. They are expected to know about different ways that people solve their problems. You will learn about many different options available to people for solving many different types of problems. You will also learn how to help clients consider the pros and cons of such options. In sum, you can expect to learn the skills useful in helping people solve their problems.

WHAT WILL BE EXPECTED FROM YOU?

The training lessons are designed so that you will learn one counseling skill at a time. The lessons contain information about why, when, and how to use each helping skill. You will be expected to read and learn this material.

You will also be expected to practice the helping skills with another person. It will be to your best advantage to practice these new skills as often as possible. The more you practice them, the more natural they will seem to you. As the skills seem more and more natural, people may regard you as a more genuine and warm person.

You will also be expected to demonstrate mastery of one counseling skill before proceeding to the next. Since all of the skills are critical to helping others, it is important for you to be able to use all of them well. You will be given feedback about your skill development so that you can learn each skill to perfection. We prefer that you move slowly and learn each skill well. If you rush through the material, you may find yourself unable to know what to say to someone requesting help.

HOW MUCH TIME WILL BE REQUIRED?

The length of time required for training will vary for each student since each of us reads and learns at a different rate. Your learning will come primarily from studying and practicing. Usually, the amount of studying time for these lessons varies from about four to fifteen hours.

Each student will also need differing lengths of time to practice each skill before really mastering it. You will probably find some skills easier to learn than others. Don't be surprised if others find different skills harder or easier to learn than you do. Everyone is different. The more students are willing to practice on their own and with their friends, the less time they probably will require in actual classroom training. Practice time usually averages between eight and twenty hours. So, the total amount of time required for the training might be between twelve and thirty-five hours. But we strongly encourage you to practice as much as you can. When you talk with a real client, you'll be glad to be well practiced and to know exactly what to do.

THINGS TO TALK OVER WITH THE INSTRUCTOR

The instructor is available to help you learn the counseling skills. Often, newly trained helpers have questions about when to use various counseling skills. Although much of this information is explained in each chapter, you should bring up your questions with the instructor. As you learn more and more of the counseling skills, new questions may arise. For example, you may wonder which of several possible skills is most appropriate for certain counseling situations. If you have any questions about when or how to use a counseling skill, talk with your instructor.

It also sometimes happens that a new helper will feel uncomfortable in encouraging another person to talk about feelings. Many of us are not used to this kind of talk and feel nervous or embarrassed. You may even feel that you are invading a person's privacy by encouraging talk about that person's feelings. It is important for you to know that you will not be taught how to *force* someone to say something; that is not what helping is about. You will learn that clients find it helpful to be given an opportunity to talk about their feelings with someone who is not a family member or friend. Because we know that talking about feelings can clarify problem situations and make it easier for clients to choose a course of action, we encourage you to tolerate any initial feelings of discomfort when listening to people share their feelings and private thoughts.

Most helpers get over this feeling of discomfort in time. With experience, you will learn how useful this conversation is to the client. If you feel discomfort or embarrassment while talking with clients, see if it goes away after you master most of the counseling skills. If it does not go away, these concerns may interfere with your ability to listen closely and to be an effective helper. Accordingly, it may be helpful for you to discuss this with your instructor to see if he or she can help you overcome these feelings.

PART II

THE TRAINING LESSONS

4

The Skilled Helper at Work

A COMPLETE EXAMPLE OF A COUNSELOR HELPING A CLIENT

Read and study this example of a skilled helper during an interview with a client. The helping skills used in each exchange appear to the right of the dialogue. The upcoming lessons will provide instruction and training in each of these counseling and problem-solving skills.

HELPER: Hello, Mrs. Wilson. My name is Cynthia Thompson. Won't you please come with me? My office is in here.
CLIENT: Thank you.

Invite client into office

HELPER: Have a seat, please. How are you today?
CLIENT: O.K.

Exchange initial greetings

HELPER: It's a beautiful fall day today, isn't it?
CLIENT: Oh yes, it's just beautiful.

HELPER: Let me explain that what we talk about will be kept confidential and just between the two of us.
CLIENT: Oh. That's good to know.

Explain confidentiality

HELPER: Uh-huh.
CLIENT: I've never talked to a counselor before.

HELPER: I imagine you must be a little nervous, then, about being here.
CLIENT: You're right.

Reflecting statement

HELPER: What seems to be the problem?
CLIENT: It's hard to know where to start. Well, the most immediate problem is that my daughter ran away from home.

Request problem statement

HELPER: I see.
CLIENT: She's back home again now. The police found her, but I'm worried she'll try running away again.

Verbal encouragement

HELPER: Uh-huh.	Verbal
CLIENT: You see, we've had problems with her since she was a little girl. She's never run away before, but I can't really say I'm surprised she tried.	encouragement
HELPER: Uh-huh.	Verbal
CLIENT: I think I've been a good mother and everything, don't misunderstand me. It's just . . . well, it's just that she never has been a very happy child.	encouragement
HELPER: It sounds like you have feelings that maybe you've been doing something that has been keeping her from being happy.	Reflecting statement
CLIENT: Yeah, I do. I've tried to provide for her and love her. Sometimes I let things get to me a little too much, though.	
HELPER: What do you mean by that?	Open-ended
CLIENT: I guess I let things make me mad when really they aren't that important.	question
HELPER: Could you give me an example of how that happens?	Closed-ended
CLIENT: Let's see. Um . . . well, for instance, the day before Kathy ran away I had had a bad day at work, and the house was a mess when I got home. I pretty much exploded at Kathy about the mess. She was supposed to have the house cleaned by the time I got home from work, but I guess I didn't have to get quite so mad at her.	question
HELPER: Especially since she ran away, I guess you feel a bit guilty about getting so mad.	Reflecting statement
CLIENT: That's exactly right. It's just been so hard for me raising her by myself since my husband died.	
HELPER: Uh-huh.	Verbal
CLIENT: I get so tired between working and raising a daughter and everything else I have to do. I don't know how women with several children to raise do it.	encouragement
HELPER: I understand.	Verbal
CLIENT: I guess what's really been bothering me is that I can't blame Kathy for running away.	encouragement
HELPER: Mrs. Wilson, you seem to have some feelings about that.	Reflecting statement
CLIENT: I do. I mean, if I were her and someone was always yelling at me, I'd think about running away, too. (*Pauses*) The problem really seems to be me.	
HELPER: You sound sad as you say that.	Reflecting statement
CLIENT: Well, it's not easy to admit it. I've been so unhappy recently, but now it's ruining my relationship with my daughter. I can't let this keep happening.	

HELPER: So the problem is your own unhappiness. Is that right?	Define the problem
CLIENT: That's right.	
HELPER: Mrs. Wilson, let's try to solve your problem by thinking of all the different things you can do to change your situation. By thinking of all the alternatives we can, you can think about the pros and cons of each one and make the best decision about what to do. Most people find it very useful to do this before making a decision.	Explain problem-solving process
CLIENT: That sounds all right.	
HELPER: Let's see what alternatives we can think of to help you with your problem. I'm going to write them down so we remember all of them. What ideas do you have?	Identify alternative solutions
CLIENT: It's funny because I thought the problem was my daughter, and now I'm thinking of ways for *my* life to be happier. But that is where the problem really is.	
HELPER: Uh-huh.	Verbal encouragement
CLIENT: Thinking about what I can do for myself. Boy, that's a new thing for me to think about.	
HELPER: What are some things you can do for yourself?	Open-ended question
CLIENT: I could make a point of going out more. I stay home too much.	
HELPER: Uh-huh.	Verbal encouragement
CLIENT: I need to do more in life than work and come home.	
HELPER: What other things could you do?	Open-ended question
CLIENT: I could entertain more in my home.	
HELPER: Uh-huh.	Verbal encouragement
CLIENT: I used to love to have guests, but since Howard died, I really haven't done any entertaining.	
HELPER: What other ideas do you have?	Open-ended question
CLIENT: Um...I don't know. I can't think of anything else.	
HELPER: How about contacting your church? They often have social events, and you might find them enjoyable.	Identify alternative solutions
CLIENT: That's a good idea. I like some of the people in the congregation real well. Actually, I haven't been going to church for the past several weeks because I just haven't been doing anything at all recently.	
HELPER: But it seems like you're ready to change that.	Reflecting statement
CLIENT: I am.	
HELPER: What other solutions can you think of?	Open-ended question
CLIENT: Um...	

(Dialogue continues on page 14.)

HELPER: Have you thought about talking to a professional counselor about your problems with your daughter and your general unhappy feelings?	Identify alternative solutions
CLIENT: Hm...no, I hadn't thought of that. Actually, that might be just what I need.	
HELPER: Can you think of anything else you could do?	Identify alternative solutions
CLIENT: Um...maybe I could find a hobby.	
HELPER: Can you think of any others?	Closed-ended question
CLIENT: No, I can't.	
HELPER: Let me think. (*Pauses*) I can't, either. So let me review all the alternatives we've thought of. You could get out more, entertain in your home, contact your church, see a professional counselor, or find a hobby. Can you think of any more?	Summarization
CLIENT: No.	
HELPER: Here's the list. Let's look at each one of these ideas and talk about what might happen if you were to choose any one of them.	Analyze consequences for each alternative
CLIENT: Okay.	
HELPER: Let's start with you getting out more. What would happen if you chose this one?	Analyze consequences
CLIENT: (*Little laugh*) Well, maybe I'd have more fun.	
HELPER: But I noticed the laugh. Maybe you're a little nervous about going out more.	Reflecting statement
CLIENT: Boy, that's pretty good. Yeah, I am nervous about it. It's been so long since I've gone out and done anything. I don't even know if I have any clothes to wear anymore.	
HELPER: Uh-huh. What else might happen?	Analyze consequences
CLIENT: Well, if I could get over the nervousness, it would probably be the best thing for me.	
HELPER: Mrs. Wilson, how would you rate this alternative? Excellent? Fair? Poor?	Rate alternative
CLIENT: It's an excellent alternative...it's just whether I could get myself to do it.	
HELPER: So you like the idea, but you feel unsure that you'd do it or not, right?	Reflecting statement
CLIENT: Right.	
HELPER: What about entertaining in your home. What might be the outcome of that?	Analyze consequences
CLIENT: That also would be good.	
HELPER: Uh-huh. What might come from it?	Open-ended question
CLIENT: I'd have some fun, maybe.	

HELPER: Uh-huh. It also might be easier for you than going out because you'd be able to invite whomever you want.

CLIENT: Good point. I don't know, though. I haven't done any entertaining in a long time.

Analyze consequences

HELPER: So it sounds like you are a little nervous about that idea, too.

CLIENT: I am.

Reflecting statement

HELPER: How would you rate the idea of entertaining at home? Excellent? Fair? Poor?

CLIENT: I'd rate it excellent. It would be a very good thing for me to do.

Rate alternative

HELPER: What about the idea of contacting your church?

CLIENT: That really might be the best. That way I would already know some of the people. Also, it's been so long since I've had people over to my house, I really would need to fix a few things up first.

Analyze consequences

HELPER: It sounds like you like this alternative.

CLIENT: I do.

Reflecting statement

HELPER: How would you rate it?

CLIENT: Excellent.

Rate alternative

HELPER: How about seeing a professional counselor?

CLIENT: I think I should do that regardless of what else I do.

Analyze consequences

HELPER: What do you see as coming from it?

CLIENT: Well, just talking to you now has made me feel much better.

Open-ended question

HELPER: Uh-huh.

CLIENT: I can even admit that the problem is not just my daughter but also me. It seems counseling would be a good thing for me now.

Verbal encouragement

HELPER: Sometimes counseling costs something.

CLIENT: I could work that out.

Analyze consequences

HELPER: Counselors also usually know people and resources in the area who can help people out, and you might find that helpful also.

CLIENT: Uh-huh.

Analyze consequences

HELPER: Sounds like you like the idea of counseling.

CLIENT: I do.

Reflecting statement

HELPER: How would you rate it?

CLIENT: Excellent.

Rate alternative

HELPER: What about finding a hobby?

CLIENT: I think the thing I don't need to do now is to spend more time by myself.

Analyze consequences

HELPER: Can you think of any advantages of finding a hobby?

CLIENT: Not really.

Analyze
consequences

HELPER: It might give you something more interesting to do when you are alone.

CLIENT: That's true.

Analyze
consequences

HELPER: How do you feel about this one?

CLIENT: It's a good idea, but the others are better.

Rate
alternative

HELPER: So you'd rate it fair?

CLIENT: That's right.

Rate
alternative

HELPER: Mrs. Wilson, here's the list of alternatives and the way you rated them. Which ones sound best?

CLIENT: I think counseling and getting involved in church should help a lot.

Select best
alternative(s)

HELPER: How do they sound?

CLIENT: Good.

Determine
client's
satisfaction

HELPER: They sound good to me, too. Do you need any help arranging counseling?

CLIENT: No thank you. I already know where to go.

Ask if help
is needed

HELPER: Good. So we talked about all the ways we could think of for you to be happier. You decided counseling would be helpful. Also, contacting the church and getting involved in social activities there would be good for you. Is that right?

CLIENT: Yes. You know, I really feel much better now that I feel like I have some direction again.

Summarization

HELPER: I'm glad. Please let me know how things work out. Is there anything else you'd like to talk about?

CLIENT: Not today.

Request feedback;
request client
questions

HELPER: Please let me know if there is anything else I can do for you.

CLIENT: Thank you. This has been very helpful.

Offer
future help

HELPER: Oh, I'm glad. It's been nice talking with you. I hope to hear from you again.

CLIENT: Thank you very much.

HELPER: Good-bye, Mrs. Wilson.

CLIENT: Bye.

Make parting
statements

5

How to Listen Actively
to a Client

ACTIVE LISTENING

Good listening skills are crucial to effective helping. Listening is an *active* process by which the helper shows respect for the client and demonstrates interest in the problems presented. Active listening encourages the client to relax and to communicate more information. More information helps the helper gain a better understanding of the client's problems. This chapter outlines the components of active listening: what to notice about the client, what to do, and what to say. Good listening is the foundation of an effective helping relationship.

When to Use

Using active listening in the following situations:

- The helper wants to encourage the client to continue talking.
- The helper begins to feel uncomfortable, and doesn't know what to do in the session.
- The helper wants to show the client that he or she is particularly interested in what the client is saying.

Listening to a client involves three components: doing, saying, and observing. As you will see in the following sections, the skilled helper *acts, talks,* and *observes* to motivate the client to provide further information.

WHAT TO DO DURING ACTIVE LISTENING

We recommend four nonverbal activities in active listening:

1. Assume an active listening posture.
2. Maintain eye contact.
3. Make active listening facial expressions.
4. Make nonverbal encouragements.

1. Assume an Active Listening Posture

- **General posture:** Your body should face the client. Lean forward slightly, sit up straight in your chair, and try not to slouch. Try not to be restless or fidgety.
- **Head:** Hold your head up straight.
- **Arms and hands:** Your arms might be on the arm rest of the chair, on the desk top, or on your lap. Place your hands on your lap or on the desk. Use your hands to gesture occasionally while you speak. Try to keep your hands away from your face; don't cross your arms. Don't play with your hair, jewelry, pen, etc.
- **Legs and feet:** Rest your feet on the floor. Try to avoid nervous leg movements.
- **In other words:** Sit still and naturally, gesture as you do when talking conversationally.

Figure 1 shows examples of appropriate and inappropriate listening postures. By assuming an active listening posture, the helper demonstrates an interest in the client's problem. It suggests a professionalism that may help build a trusting relationship with the client.

2. Maintain Eye Contact

You should look directly into the client's eyes while either you or the client is talking. Avoid staring at the client or looking with a fixed gaze or glare.

Maintaining eye contact shows a continued interest in the client. It conveys respect for what the person is saying and suggests a willingness to hear more from the client. Eye contact communicates caring.

3. Make Active Listening Facial Expressions

Use the natural facial expression that you have when paying attention. For example, you might close your mouth when the subject matter is serious or sad; smile or laugh when the discussion is happy. Chewing gum can be a distraction to someone who is trying to talk about a problem.

Figure 2 shows appropriate and inappropriate facial expressions. Facial expressions of active listening let the client know that you follow what he or she is saying and that you are taking it seriously. Facial expressions also convey attention, and thus may help to maintain the client's talking.

4. Make Nonverbal Encouragements

You might nod your head or smile while maintaining eye contact with the client.

Figure 1. Examples of Good and Bad Listening Postures

Good posture: Notice that the helper is sitting up straight and is facing the client squarely.

Bad posture: Notice that the helper is slouched in her chair with her arms crossed over her chest. This posture can make a client feel that he or she is being judged; it is not a good posture for developing a good helping relationship.

Good posture: Notice that the helper is leaning forward slightly and listening to the client talk.

Bad posture: Notice that the helper is leaning an elbow on the desk. This posture can make a client feel that he or she is boring the helper; it is not a good posture for developing a good helping relationship.

An example of nonverbal encouragements follows: As the client talks, the helper is looking at her face and into her eyes periodically. The helper's face is serious; her mouth is closed, her eyebrows and forehead wrinkled. The helper is following what the client is saying, and nods her head to let the client know.

Nonverbal encouragements are designed to acknowledge a continued interest in the client's conversation and to encourage the client to continue talking.

WHAT TO SAY DURING ACTIVE LISTENING

The only verbal activity in active listening is to make verbal encouragements. In making verbal encouragements or in any counseling conversation, try to use good verbal quality.

Make Verbal Encouragements

You should make a brief (usually not more than two-word) statement acknowledging the client's comment.

Examples of verbal encouragements are:

- "Uh-huh,"
- "Oh,"
- "Mm-hm,"
- "I see,"
- "Mm,"
- I understand."
- "Yes,"
- "Yeah,"

Verbal encouragements indicate to the client, "Go on, I'm with you. I'm listening and following you, not just sitting here because I'm supposed to." These encourage the client to continue the conversation in a direction determined by him or her. This results in more information; something essential to the helping relationship.

Use Good Verbal Quality

This involves talking in a pleasant, nonthreatening, interested intonation. The voice is neither too loud nor too soft for the setting in which the interview takes place. Bad verbal quality includes a dull, flat, bored, or quivering tone of voice; stuttering; or inappropriate laughter. Avoid excessive use of "you know," "like," or "uh." Also, avoid clearing your throat before speaking.

If the helper has good verbal and tonal quality, the client is more likely to want to continue the visit.

Read the following example of a counselor making good verbal encouragements. Notice how the helper encourages the client to continue speaking:

CLIENT: Well, I'm having this problem with my boyfriend.
HELPER: Oh?
CLIENT: I really don't know where to begin explaining how the whole thing happened.
HELPER: Uh-huh.
CLIENT: It started when we began to talk about getting married.
HELPER: I see.
CLIENT: After that, he quit coming around as often and wouldn't tell me why. I know it's because he got afraid of us talking about getting married.

Figure 2. Examples of Good and Bad Facial Expressions

Good expression: Notice that the helper is maintaining eye contact and a facial expression of active listening.

Bad expression: Notice that the helper is not maintaining eye contact. She looks bored.

WHAT TO OBSERVE DURING ACTIVE LISTENING

There are four observing (or nonverbal) activities in active listening:

1. Identify the content of the client's verbal statements.
2. Identify the client's feelings.
3. Identify the feelings of the client's verbal behavior.
4. Identify the feelings of the client's nonverbal behavior.

1. Identify the Content of the Client's Verbal Statements

You should accurately determine what the client is talking about by identifying the topics the client discusses. You can do this by asking the following questions silently to yourself:

- "What is the situation the client is talking about?"
- "Who is the client talking about?"
- "Where does this occur?"
- "When was it?" or "When will it be?"

When a counselor can identify the content of a client's statement, the counselor can begin to help the client solve his or her problem.

Read the following examples of client statements. Identify the content of each example:

EXAMPLE 1
CLIENT: My husband's drinking is ruining the whole family. The kids are afraid of him, and I'm afraid he'll lose his job.

Content: Husband's drinking. Children are afraid of their father. Husband may lose his job.

EXAMPLE 2
CLIENT: My ex-husband agreed to pay child support when we got divorced. The first month he paid it. The second month, I only got $100, and the last I heard, he's left the state, which means I'll never get anything from him. What am I going to do?

Content: Ex-husband not paying child support.

► EXERCISE 1
CLIENT: I just had my shift changed at work. Now I'm supposed to work 3 to 11. My husband doesn't come home from work until 6, and that will mean there will be no one to take care of our children until then.

Content: _____

► EXERCISE 2
CLIENT: I have a job where I have to be able to make good decisions. I have a hard time deciding what parts to buy, and I am never sure I've ordered the right parts even after I've placed the order. It's making it hard to work because I'm spending so much time wondering if I'm doing the right thing.

Content: _____

2. Identify the Client's Feelings

You should determine what the client is feeling by identifying his or her emotions as, for example, happy, mad, sad, confused, or scared. You can do this by asking yourself the following questions:

- "How would I feel if I were placed in the situation described by the client?"
- "How does the client feel?"
- "How would most people feel in that situation?"

When a counselor can identify the feelings of a client's statement, he or she can begin to understand the client's frame of reference.

Here is a list of words to describe some feelings that clients experience:

Happy	**Sad**	**Angry**	**Scared**	**Confused**
Joyous	Depressed	Furious	Fearful	Bothered
Pleased	Hopeless	Annoyed	Afraid	Undecided
Satisfied	Sorrowful	Frustrated	Insecure	Trapped
Delighted	Melancholy	Agitated	Unsure	Troubled
Glad	Dejected	Dismayed	Nervous	Mixed up

Read the following example of a client's statement. Then, identify the feeling in each exercise.

EXAMPLE

CLIENT: My husband's drinking is ruining the whole family. The kids are afraid of him and I'm worried he'll lose his job.

Feelings: Worried, upset.

▶ EXERCISE 1

CLIENT: Hey, I got that job I wanted.

Feelings: _____

▶ EXERCISE 2

CLIENT: I don't know what to do. Everything's been happening so fast. I just can't believe he would leave so fast. It seemed like things could have been worked out. I never thought he would really leave. Now what am I going to do?

Feelings: _____

▶ EXERCISE 3

CLIENT: I have a job where I have to be able to make good decisions. I have a hard time deciding what parts to buy, and am never sure I've ordered the right parts even after I've placed the order. It's making it hard to work because I'm spending so much time wondering if I'm doing the right thing.

Feelings: _____

▶ EXERCISE 4

CLIENT: It just seems like I don't do things as well as everyone else.

Feelings: _____

(Exercises continue on page 24.)

► **EXERCISE 5**

CLIENT: I've been spending a lot of time at home watching TV. I guess it's kind of boring, but I'm not really interested in doing anything else. I mean, I have friends and everything, but I never feel like doing what they are doing. I wish I had something to do.

Feelings: _____

► **EXERCISE 6**

CLIENT: All my friends can stay out until one o'clock and I have to be in at twelve. My parents are so unfair.

Feelings: _____

► **EXERCISE 7**

CLIENT: Everything's a mess. Not only has my telephone been turned off, but they might turn off the water now. I try to pay the rent on time, but sometimes the other bills come in, and I can't help getting behind on some of them.

Feelings: _____

► **EXERCISE 8**

CLIENT: I basically don't give a damn anymore.

Feelings: _____

► **EXERCISE 9**

CLIENT: Do you think they'll ever find out it was me? I mean, if my sister ever tells them...boy, that would be a bad scene.

Feelings: _____

3. Identify the Feelings of the Client's Verbal Behavior

You should observe the tone of voice, loudness or softness, spacing of words, speed of speech, any stuttering, emphasis of particular words or phrases, pauses, any emotional outlets such as crying, laughing, sighs, and silences. You should identify the feeling noted in the client's voice as, for example, happy, sad, mad, confused, or scared. You can do this by asking yourself the following questions:

- "How do I usually feel when I speak in that tone of voice?"
- "How do most people feel when they speak in that tone of voice?"

By noticing the client's verbal behavior, the helper gets much more information than he or she would by just listening to the words spoken. The tone of voice can either match the content or be in conflict with it. Being able to identify when the client's verbal statements are in agreement or disagreement with his or her feelings will be important in helping a client clearly identify the problem and decide upon ways to change the situation.

Here is a list of some verbal behaviors and the feelings they frequently indicate:

Verbal Behavior	Feeling
Crying	Sadness, upset, frustration
Loud or yelling voice	Anger
Soft voice	Fear, sadness
Pause and then sigh	Confusion, depression, frustration
Talking very quickly	Nervousness, fear, excitement
Talking very slowly	Sadness, depression
Laughing	Happiness, nervousness
Silences	Nervousness, depression, confusion

4. Identify the Feelings of the Client's Nonverbal Behavior

You should observe the client's body movements and posture. Notice what the client does with his or her hands, legs, arms, and face. What is the facial expression—a smile, frown, grimace, or some other? Observe whether the client moves frequently or sits still during the session. Observe whether or not the client is making eye contact. You should identify the feeling noted in the client's facial expressions as, for example, happy, sad, mad, confused, scared, or nervous. You can do this by asking yourself the following questions:

- "How do I usually feel when I act nonverbally the way the client is now?"

- "How do most people feel when they are acting nonverbally the way the client is now?"

Observing the client's gestures ("body language") during the session gives the helper more information about how the client feels toward whatever is being discussed. Understanding how the client is feeling may help you be a more empathic and understanding helper.

Here is a list of some body movements and the feelings they frequently indicate:

Body Movement	Feeling
Trembling fingers	Nervousness, fear
Repeated folding and unfolding hands	Nervousness, fear
Tapping fingers on table	Nervousness, fear
Tapping feet on floor	Nervousness, boredom
Swinging leg over knee repeatedly	Nervousness, fear
Shaking foot back and forth	Nervousness
Shoulder pulled forward, head leaning down, eyes to floor	Sadness, depression
Fingers held in a fist	Anger
Pounding hand or fist on table	Anger
Stomping foot on floor	Anger
Raising shoulders toward ears	Confusion

Noting the feelings indicated by body movements provides information that can be shared with the client. Comparing the feelings suggested by the client's verbal behavior and body language provides a basis for making a reflection statement (about which you will learn more in the next chapter). Pointing out to a client any inconsistencies between his or her verbal statements, verbal behavior, and body language can be helpful because it can help reduce any confusion the client may have about what to do.

Read the following examples of client statements. Below some of the examples are descriptions of the verbal behavior used by the client. Where it is not described, identify the behavior, and identify the feeling of the client in each example.

EXAMPLE
CLIENT: I've just about had it.

Verbal Behavior: Loud voice, fast speech.
Feelings: Angry, disgusted.

► EXERCISE 1
CLIENT: It just seems like I don't do things as well as everyone else.

Verbal Behavior: Slow speech.

Feelings: _____

► EXERCISE 2
CLIENT: So the next thing I did was run next door and make sure everyone was okay. I mean, it was so loud.

Verbal Behavior: Fast speech.

Feelings: _____

► EXERCISE 3
CLIENT: (*Giggle*) It sounds so stupid to talk about.

Verbal Behavior: _____

Feelings: _____

► EXERCISE 4
CLIENT: It all gets so confusing. I don't even know where to begin . . . . (*3-4 second pause*) Uh, where should I start?

Verbal Behavior: _____

Feelings: _____

SUMMARY

In summary, there are three components of active listening:

1. doing (nonverbal activity),
2. saying (verbal activity), and
3. observing (nonverbal activity).

Doing

1. Assume an appropriate posture.
2. Maintain eye contact with the client.
3. Make appropriate facial expressions.
4. Make nonverbal encouragements.

Saying

1. Make verbal encouragement (for example, "uh-huh").

Observing

1. Identify the content of the client's verbal statements.
2. Identify the client's feelings.
3. Identify the feelings of client's verbal behavior.
4. Identify the feelings of client's nonverbal behavior.

STUDY GUIDE

REVIEW QUESTIONS

Make sure you can answer all of the following questions. If you are unable to answer any question, reread the appropriate section of the chapter, and try the question again. It will be important that you know this information before beginning the practice sessions.

1. When is it particularly important to use active listening?
2. What are the three components of active listening?
3. There are four activities involved in the doing component of active listening.
   - What are they?
   - What does each activity involve?
4. There is only one verbal activity involved in the saying component of active listening.
   - What is it?
   - What does it involve?
5. There are four activities involved in the observing component of active listening.
   - What are they?
   - What does each activity involve?
6. Why is active listening so important to good counseling?

(Study Guide continues on page 28.)

SKILLS PRACTICE

Here are an example and several exercises in which a student and a partner can practice the skill of active listening. For additional practice, you can create your own situations.

Role playing involves trying to create a situation in which the helper actually counsels a client with problems. The student should try to do his or her best in counseling the partner playing the role of a client. The partner should try his or her best to act out the situation in a realistic way. Here is an example of how a partner might role play a problem situation to provide practice for this skill:

EXAMPLE

CLIENT (Partner): My daughter is having trouble keeping up with the school work. (*Pauses*)

HELPER (Student): *Should have good posture, eye contact, facial expression, and make verbal and nonverbal encouragements.*

CLIENT: *Uses the Skills Checklist to check the things that went well and the things that need improvement.*

SAMPLE SKILLS CHECKLIST

Skill

Practice Session Number

1 2 3 4 5 6 7 8 9 10

Posture
Eye contact
Facial expression
Nonverbal encouragements
Verbal encouragements

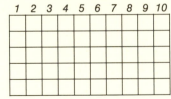

✓ = well done;   o = needs work

After completing the Skills Checklist, the partner tells the student the things that went well. (For example, "Your posture and eye contact were excellent.")

The things that need improvement are then described to the student. (For example, "Let's try to practice the verbal and nonverbal encouragements. Okay?")

Each student should practice the skill in role-playing situations until he or she is able to use the skill perfectly. The partner should use the Skills Checklist to check the things that are done well and the things that need improvement. We recommend that you practice until two practice sessions are done perfectly or until you feel comfortable with the skill. Then you will be ready for the Quality Check.

 EXERCISE 1

The union you belong to just voted to strike. You are angry because that will mean financial hardships for you and your family during the strike.

SKILLS CHECKLIST

Skill

Posture
Eye contact
Facial expression
Nonverbal encouragements
Verbal encouragements

Practice Session Number

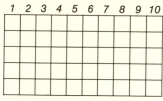

✔ = well done;   o = needs work

▶ **EXERCISE 2**

You are a teenager who has come to the counselor for advice. You parents are always fighting. You think it would be better if they got divorced, but you don't know how to tell them this.

▶ **EXERCISE 3**

You are feeling lonely and depressed. You came to the counselor for help.

▶ **EXERCISE 4**

You don't like your present job, and would like to find a new one. You are hoping the counselor will be able to help you.

6

How to Reflect
a Client's Verbal
and Nonverbal Behavior

Usually, people coming for help are confused about what to do. Reflecting a client's verbal and nonverbal behavior is an important counseling skill designed to help a client gain a clearer understanding of his or her feelings. In reflecting verbal and nonverbal behavior, the helper points out aspects of the client's behavior and feelings. The message to the client is one of sincere interest and support: "I am listening closely to you, and want to share with you what I am observing to help you solve your problem." Accurate reflection is an important counseling skill to help a client solve a problem. This chapter outlines the components of making good reflecting statements.

Read these complete examples of a helper and client in a counseling session. They demonstrate how the helper reflects the client's verbal and nonverbal behavior.

EXAMPLE 1

HELPER: What seems to be the problem?

CLIENT: I have lots of problems. (*Little nervous laugh*) It's strange, but I don't know how to begin. (*Nervous laugh*) Oh, how strange. (*Little laugh*)

HELPER: Steve, you sound like you're feeling nervous about being here.

CLIENT: Oh, I am! I wanted to come here, but now that I'm here, I don't know where to begin. Ah, saying it makes me feel better. Okay. Now I'm ready to talk. Yeah, I am nervous. I've never talked to a counselor before.

EXAMPLE 2

CLIENT: It's gotten worse. (*5-second pause; continues in softer tone of voice*) As a matter of fact, it's gotten much worse.

HELPER: I noticed you sound depressed.

CLIENT: Oh yeah. (*Pauses*) I've been feeling so down all week. I don't know what's going to happen.

HELPER: Uh-huh.

CLIENT: There's another thing though. (*Louder tone of voice*) Oh, it's so unfair!

HELPER: What other thing are you talking about?

CLIENT: My boss.

HELPER: It seems like you're mad about whatever's been going on with your boss.

CLIENT: You're right. It makes me furious.

When to Use

Use reflecting statements in the following situations:

- The helper observes a sudden change in the client's verbal behavior. Examples: starts to cry, suddenly stops talking altogether, begins talking much louder, begins talking much softer, suddenly speaks in angry tone, suddenly changes voice tone to calmness or laughter.

- The helper observes a sudden change in the client's nonverbal behavior. Examples: suddenly gets out of chair, suddenly pounds fist, clenches fist, or makes a dramatic change in the way he or she is sitting, breaks eye contact for an extended time.

- The helper observes a difference between the client's verbal statements and the feelings of his or her verbal or nonverbal behavior. Example: your client might say, "I'm not worried about it," while shaking his or her foot back and forth nervously.

- The helper can identify the feelings expressed by the client's verbal statements and nonverbal behavior. This is particularly important to do in two situations:

  1. while the client is describing his or her problem, and

  2. while the client is considering the consequences of the alternative solutions available to solve his or her problem.

Read the following examples of client statements. Identify those examples for which it would be appropriate to make a reflecting statement, and explain why the chosen examples would call for a reflecting statement.

EXAMPLE 1

CLIENT: I'm a senior in high school. I've always done well in school, but recently it hasn't been interesting me at all. (*4-second pause; depressed tone*) Oh, I don't know what I want to do anymore.

Reflect because: There was a change in verbal behavior.

EXAMPLE 2

CLIENT: It is kind of complicated, but I need help figuring out what to do about my job. I feel like I'm being discriminated against, and I don't know what to do. It's really terrible because I know I should do something about it, but I'm afraid if I do tell someone what's been going on, I'll lose my job, and then I'll really have a problem. Do you think you can help me figure out what to do?

Reflect because: Counselor identified feelings while client described the problem.

(Exercises are on page 32.)

▶ **EXERCISE 1**

CLIENT: My mother has been sick for the past couple of years. It's been very hard on all of us because she needs a lot of care, and that takes a lot of time. It's really terrible to say that your mother is a burden, isn't it?

Reflect because: _____

▶ **EXERCISE 2**

CLIENT: (*Angry tone of voice*) Oh! This thing is such a nuisance! (*Softer*) Of course, I really don't let it get to me.

Reflect because: _____

▶ **EXERCISE 3**

CLIENT: I've been feeling so down recently. I'm not even sure this counseling will help, but there was nothing else I could think of doing. I don't know what's been bothering me, really, just feeling down.

Reflect because: _____

▶ **EXERCISE 4**

CLIENT: (*Speaking slowly, in a depressed tone*) That's a good idea.

Reflect because: _____

We recommend two activities in reflecting a client's verbal and nonverbal behavior:

1. making a reflecting statement, and

2. pausing after the reflecting statement.

1. Make a Reflecting Statement

You should use an appropriate initial phrase, include a feeling or noticing statement about the client's verbal statement or verbal or nonverbal behavior, use an appropriate facial expression of seriousness and concern, lean slightly forward, and maintain eye contact with the client.

Examples of appropriate initial phrases include:

- "I noticed you . . ."
- "You sound like you feel . . ."
- "You look like you feel . . ."
- "I imagine you feel . . ."
- "It sounds like . . ."
- "It sounds like that makes you feel . . ."
- "As I listen to you, I sense that you might be feeling . . ."
- "As I listen to you, I notice that . . ."

Beginning a reflecting statement with one of these initial phrases tells the client that you are trying to participate in his or her experience, and to understand the situation. This sharing of feelings helps build the trust essential to an effective helping relationship.

In the following examples, the helper makes reflecting statements.

EXAMPLE 1

CLIENT: The family gets long well. We used to go on wonderful family vacations—swimming, camping, lots of barbecuing. John, my oldest son, is a great outdoor chef. We haven't done that in a long time. (*Long pause; proceeds in a sad tone of voice*) Our daughter . . . well, she won't do anything with the family anymore.

HELPER: That thought seems to make you feel sad. (*Reflecting statement*)

CLIENT: It makes me sadder than I even realized. You know . . . .

EXAMPLE 2

CLIENT: My wife is always spending my money. She charges everything, and it's gotten to the point where my credit is going to be worthless unless she cuts it out. I've tried everything to stop her, but now I really think she has a problem. I mean, nothing has worked, and I think she has a serious problem controlling herself from buying things.

HELPER: I see.

CLIENT: (*Proceeds in a loud voice*) Who does she think she is anyway? I work hard for that money, and now we are almost broke because of her carelessness.

HELPER: You sound very angry about the situation. (*Reflecting statement*)

CLIENT: I guess I am. I hate admitting I am so mad at my wife because I really think there is something wrong with her, but I have just about had it.

EXAMPLE 3

CLIENT: My mother-in-law has moved into our house recently. I never wanted her to come in the first place, but her husband died a couple of years ago, and she just hasn't been able to afford keeping up their old house. My wife insisted, so in she moved. My wife loves having her mother around—it's like she's become a little girl again. (*Slumps down in chair, leans head back, and breaks eye contact.*) I'm losing my wife. She doesn't do anything I ask her to anymore. It's like being totally out of control in your own home.

HELPER: You look like you are feeling depressed about it. (*Reflecting statement*)

CLIENT: Yeah.

2. Pause after the Reflecting Statement

You should sit in a relaxed position and face the client with your eyes focused on his or her face. Assume a posture for active listening. You should not say anything for at least five seconds.

Waiting in silence after making a reflecting statement allows the client time to think about your observation and make a further comment. The pause shows the client that you are listening and that you want him or her to continue talking.

As a guide to putting it all together, we have included the following exercises. Read each exercise, make an appropriate reflecting statement, and pause.

▶ **EXERCISE 1**

CLIENT: I've been feeling so down recently. I'm not even sure this counseling will help, but there was nothing else I could think of doing. I don't know what's been bothering me, really...I'm just feeling down.

HELPER: _____

▶ **EXERCISE 2**

CLIENT: (*Slowly; sounding depressed*) That's a good idea.

HELPER: _____

▶ **EXERCISE 3**

HELPER: How would you describe your problem?
CLIENT: I've lost my job and need help finding a new one. Can you help?
HELPER: What happened with your last job?
CLIENT: Well, I missed work a few times and got fired.
HELPER: How come you missed work?
CLIENT: (*Little laugh*) Well (*little laugh*) you see, well, uh, I just overslept a few times.

HELPER: _____ (*Pauses*)

CLIENT: Well, you know, people might get the wrong idea.
HELPER: What do you mean by that?
CLIENT: Well, it might make you think I'm a bad worker or something, but things were going on that caused me to oversleep.
HELPER: Oh?
CLIENT: You see, my wife and I have been having some problems. Actually, I'm not even really living there anymore. I try to come home after everyone is asleep so I don't have to see her. But it's making me miss work in the morning. (*Pauses*) Oh... (*Sighs*)

HELPER: _____ (*Pauses*)

CLIENT: It's really such a bad thing for everyone. I would do anything if I could just run away from the fighting, but that would do nothing for my children. Of course, I'm not doing much for them now either.

HELPER: _____ (*Pauses*)

CLIENT: Yeah, I do. I can't help worrying about what all this is doing to them.

EXERCISE 4

HELPER: So what we've thought of is either continued counseling for you, or having your daughter see a counselor, or just ignoring the problem. Can you think of anything else?

CLIENT: No.

HELPER: I can think of one more thing. How about asking Sharon's teacher if she can help you and Sharon solve this problem?

CLIENT: That's a good idea.

HELPER: Now let's talk about each idea and see what might happen if you were to do it.

CLIENT: Okay.

HELPER: What do you think might happen if you continued in counseling, yourself?

CLIENT: It really has been good for me, but it hasn't helped things with my daughter very much.

HELPER: How so?

CLIENT: I've spent all of the time working on things about myself, and things with her haven't gotten talked about too much.

HELPER: Do you think your counseling might be able to help the situation between you and your daughter?

CLIENT: (*Pauses*) Well…(*Pauses*) I don't know.

HELPER: _____

CLIENT: Yes, that's right.

HELPER: How about the idea of Sharon seeing a counselor?

CLIENT: Well, all I know is that counseling helped me a lot.

HELPER: _____

CLIENT: I've really enjoyed being in counseling. Maybe if Sharon has someone to talk to about things, our situation would be better because she'd be feeling better in general.

HELPER: Uh-huh. What about ignoring the problem?

CLIENT: I just can't ignore it anymore!

HELPER: _____

CLIENT: Yes, I did. It is driving me crazy, and I can't stand it anymore.

HELPER: What about talking to Sharon's teacher?

CLIENT: I know Sharon really likes her. Maybe she'll listen to her. Sounds like it's worth a try.

HELPER: _____

SUMMARY

There are two activities in reflecting a client's verbal and nonverbal behavior:

1. Make a reflecting statement.
2. Pause after making the reflecting statement.

(Study Guide begins on page 36.)

STUDY GUIDE

REVIEW QUESTIONS

Make sure you can answer all of the following questions. If you are unable to answer any question, reread that section of the chapter, and try the question again. It will be important that you know this information before beginning the practice sessions.

1. When is it particularly important to reflect a client's verbal and nonverbal behavior?

2. There are two activities in making a reflecting statement.
   - What are they?
   - What does each step involve?

3. Why is reflecting a client's verbal and nonverbal behavior such an important counseling skill?

SKILLS PRACTICE

Here are an example and several exercises in which a student and a partner can practice the skill of reflecting. For additional practice, you can create your own situations.

Each student should practice the reflecting statements in role-playing situations until he or she is able to use this skill perfectly. The partner should use the Skills Checklist to identify things that are done well and things that need improvement. We recommend that you practice until two practice situations are done perfectly or until you feel comfortable with the skill. Then you will be ready for the Quality Check.

Here is an example of how a partner might role play a problem situation to provide practice for this skill:

EXAMPLE

CLIENT (Partner): Everything seems like such a mess.

HELPER (Student): *Should have good posture, eye contact, and facial expression, and should make verbal and nonverbal encouragements.*

CLIENT: Oh (*sighs*), it's been going on for so long.

HELPER: You sound pretty down about the whole situation.

CLIENT: *Uses the Skills Checklist to identify things that went well and things that need improving.*

▶ **EXERCISE 1**
Your father died recently, and you feel your life has changed since his death. You've come for help in getting yourself "back to normal."

▶ **EXERCISE 2**
You have recently had a bad fight with your spouse and are upset. You don't know whether or not you want to stay married any longer. You've come for help because the situation has you confused and depressed.

SKILLS CHECKLIST

Skill	Practice Session Number									
	1	2	3	4	5	6	7	8	9	10
Reflecting statements and pauses										
Active listening										
Posture										
Eye contact										
Facial expression										
Nonverbal encouragements										
Verbal encouragements										

✓ = well done;　o = needs work

EXERCISE 3

You are a high school student doing poorly in one of your classes. You have tried to improve your grade, but have been unsuccessful. Your parents will punish you if you don't improve the grade. You don't know what to do.

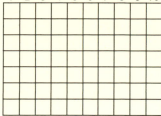

EXERCISE 4

You are looking for a job, and have filled out many applications. Each time, the employer tells you he or she will call you back, but you never receive a response. You are frustrated.

7

How to Ask
a Client Questions

Active listening, as a method of encouraging the client to share more information, has already been discussed. Asking questions is a second method of maintaining client conversation, and is the topic of this chapter. We need specific information and feedback from clients to help them, so being able to ask good questions is an essential skill for a skilled helper.

There are two types of questions used by effective helpers: open-ended questions and closed-ended questions. Each will be discussed below.

Open-ended questions are exploratory. They encourage a client to think about his or her feelings and thoughts. They are usually answered with more than one or two words. The counselor cannot predict the answer that the client will give. Open-ended questions are designed to help a client verbally explore and, it is to be hoped, clarify ideas and feelings that relate to his or her problems.

A closed-ended question, in contrast, usually asks for factual information and can often be answered with a "yes," a "no," or some other one- or two-word answer. Generally, closed-ended questions are appropriate for obtaining specific information about the client (for example: occupation, education, marital status, number of children). Besides providing factual information, however, the answers to closed-ended questions can tell a helper if his or her understanding of the content or feelings of the client's verbal statements is correct.

OPEN-ENDED QUESTIONS

Good questions are short and direct. Good question askers ask only one question at a time and do not have to explain their questions. They wait for an answer and do not answer their own questions.

When to Use

Use open-ended questions in the following situations:

- Beginning a counseling session. For example:
  - "What would you like to talk about today?"
  - "How can I help you?"

- Asking for a statement of the problem. For example:

  –"What seems to be the problem?"

- Asking for examples of specific behavior to give the helper a better understanding of what is being described. For example:

  –"What do you mean when you say she's mean?"

  –"What would be an example of that?"

- The counselor notices a sudden change in verbal or nonverbal behavior in the client, and cannot identify the feeling. For example:

  –"What are you feeling as we talk about this?"

  –"How are you reacting to talking about this?"

- The client is talking about a number of different topics, and the counselor wants to refocus the topic back to the identified problem. For example:

  –"You stated that your original concern was your daughter's irresponsible behavior. What are your thoughts about that?"

  –"Let's continue talking about the problem. How have you tried to solve it?"

- Defining the alternatives available for solving the problem. For example:

  –"What are the alternatives you've thought of?"

  –"Have you thought of . . . . "

- Asking the client about each alternative. For example:

  –"How does that sound?"

  –"What do you think of this?"

- Asking the client about his or her satisfaction with the decision he or she made. For example:

  –"What do you think about the outcome?"

  –"How does that sound?"

Read the following examples of good and bad open-ended questions. Notice that good questions are short and direct. Also notice that asking good questions means asking one question at a time. Rate each question as to whether it is good or bad, and explain why the rating is given.

EXAMPLE 1

CLIENT: She acts crazy all the time.
HELPER: What do you mean when you say she acts crazy?

Rating and reason: Good question because it was short and direct

EXAMPLE 2

CLIENT: She acts crazy all the time.
HELPER: What do you mean by crazy? I mean, there are lots of different meanings for that word, and I'm wondering what you mean by it. I mean,

I have to know what you mean so I can understand what you're talking about. I imagine you mean she does strange things, but I'm not sure. What do you mean?

Rating and reason: Bad question because it was too long, and asker answers own question

► **EXERCISE 1**

CLIENT: I need help finding a job.
HELPER: How have you already tried to find a job?

Rating and reason: _____

► **EXERCISE 2**

CLIENT: It makes me so mad.
HELPER: What makes you so mad?

Rating and reason: _____

We recommend three activities in asking an open-ended question:

1. Make an open-ended question.
2. Listen actively.
3. Make verbal or nonverbal encouragements when the client answers.

1. Make an Open-Ended Question

You should ask for information using an appropriate initial phrase; then you should pause, making no verbal statements following the end of your question. Some examples of *appropriate* initial phrases include:

- "How...?"
- "What...?"
- "How do you feel about...?"
- "Could you tell me more about...?"
- "Would you tell me more about...?"

The following are examples of *inappropriate* initial phrases for asking open-ended questions: "When...?" "Do you...?" "Why...?" "Who...?" "Where...?"
 Notice that the appropriate initial phrases for asking open-ended questions require more than a single-word answer. In contrast, the phrases in the second list can be answered merely with a "yes," "no," "because," or some other one- or two-word answer.

2. Listen Actively

You should maintain eye contact. Keep a straight face, and don't smile. Lean forward slightly while asking the question.

By listening actively you let the client know you are sincere in your questioning. It communicates that you intend to provide your best help in solving the client's problem.

3. Make Verbal or Nonverbal Encouragements When the Client Answers

You should verbally and/or nonverbally encourage the client by making a verbal encouragement such as "uh-huh" or "I see" or a nonverbal encouragement such as a head nod or smile.

Some examples of making verbal and nonverbal encouragements when the client answers the question are as follows:

EXAMPLE 1

CLIENT: (*Talking about her teacher*) She's very unfair. She's always picking on me, and it's not always me doing it.

HELPER: How does she always pick on you?

CLIENT: Well, if there is any noise in the classroom, she'll automatically call out my name to stop talking.

HELPER: I see.

CLIENT: And then if there's ever a fight, she'll always say I started it.

HELPER: Uh-huh.

EXAMPLE 2

CLIENT: I've been very unhappy at work these days.

HELPER: What have you thought about doing about it?

CLIENT: I would really like to quit.

HELPER: (*With facial expression showing interest*) Oh?

CLIENT: Yeah, I've had it.

HELPER: (*Nods head once*)

CLIENT: The boss . . . .

Read the following examples of client statements. Ask an open-ended question following each statement to obtain more information about the situation.

▶ **EXERCISE 1**

CLIENT: I'm glad I could talk to someone today. It's been an unbelievable week.

HELPER: _____

▶ **EXERCISE 2**

CLIENT: My problem is simple. I need a job.

HELPER: _____

(Exercises continue on page 42.)

▶ **EXERCISE 3**

CLIENT: The problem is that my wife won't work, and without additional money from her working we don't have enough to live on. My mother used to work. My aunt, who's 67 years old, still works to help support herself. I think it's terrible when people get so lazy and expect others to take care of them. We're not rich or anything. Even if I were rich, I'd want my wife to be willing to help out if I asked her to.

HELPER: _____

▶ **EXERCISE 4**

CLIENT: What do you want me to tell you?
HELPER: _____

▶ **EXERCISE 5**

CLIENT: The problem is that my son is flunking out of school. His father is dead, and it's been so hard for me to raise him alone. I mean, I have a full-time job, and really was never too good in school myself. The boy always went to his father when he needed help with his school work. Then there's the problem of my mother.

HELPER: _____

SUMMARY OF OPEN-ENDED QUESTIONING

In summary, the steps in asking an open-ended question are:

1. Make an open-ended question.

2. Listen actively.

3. Make verbal and nonverbal encouragements when the client answers.

CLOSED-ENDED QUESTIONS

Closed-ended questions are appropriate whenever counselors seek factual information. They are also useful when counselors want to make sure they are clearly understanding the content of the client's verbal statements.

When to Use

Use closed-ended questions in the following situations:

• Needing specific information. For example:

CLIENT: I want to register to vote, but don't know where to go.
HELPER: Where do you live?
CLIENT: I live on Seventeenth Street.

• Wanting feedback on your understanding because you are confused by the content of the client's statement. For example:

CLIENT: At first I was thinking of leaving, and left for a couple of days. But I knew that probably wouldn't solve our problem, so I moved back. I still am thinking of getting a divorce, though. I never can be the same again.

HELPER: I'm not sure I'm understanding this correctly. Is it that you've tried leaving him but knew that wouldn't solve the problem and now are thinking about getting a divorce?

CLIENT: Yep, I just can't see our marriage ever getting any better.

- Asking for confirmation of your understanding of the problem. For example:

CLIENT: I've answered every ad in the newspaper I was qualified for, and still don't have a job. I must have filled out 15 applications in the last week. Maybe you can help me figure out why I can't get a job.

HELPER: So you'd like us to work together to try to find out why you haven't gotten a job yet. Right?

CLIENT: That's right.

- Scheduling the next appointment. For example:

HELPER: When would you like to come in again?

CLIENT: Tomorrow, same time.

We recommend three activities in asking a closed-ended question:

1. Make a closed-ended question.

2. Listen actively.

3. Make verbal and nonverbal encouragements when the client answers.

1. Make a Closed-Ended Question

You should use an appropriate initial phrase; then you should pause, making no verbal statements following the end of your question.

Some examples of initial phrases include:

- "When . . . ?"
- "Who . . . ?"
- "Do you mean . . . ?"
- "Where . . . ?"
- "Are you . . . ?"
- "Is it . . . ?"

2. Listen Actively

You should maintain eye contact. Keep a straight face, and don't smile. Lean forward slightly while asking the question.

As mentioned before, listening actively communicates your intention of providing your best help in solving the client's problems.

3. Make Verbal and Nonverbal Encouragements When the Client Answers

You should encourage the client by making a verbal encouragement such as "uh-huh" or "I see" or a nonverbal encouragement such as a head nod or smile.

Two examples of making verbal and nonverbal encouragements when the client answers the question are:

- CLIENT: So that is why I've come in.
  HELPER: So it seems the problem is that your daughter has no friends in
             school and is very unhappy. Is that correct?
  CLIENT: That's it.
  HELPER: *(Nods head)* I see.

- CLIENT: Well, thank you. I think everything is taken care of.
  HELPER: Do you want to come in and talk again?
  CLIENT: I think we've gotten things pretty well settled.
  HELPER: *(Nods head once and smiles)* I'm glad.

SUMMARY OF CLOSED-ENDED QUESTIONING

In summary, the steps in asking a closed-ended question are:

1. Make a closed-ended question.

2. Listen actively.

3. Make verbal and nonverbal encouragements when the client answers.

A NOTE ABOUT "PIPE LIGHTING"

In a real counseling session, a client might make a statement in response to which it could be appropriate to make a reflecting statement, to ask an open-ended question, or to ask a closed-ended question. If you find yourself in this situation, respond in the way that feels best to *you*. Since there are helping situations in which it would be appropriate to use any of these helping skills, your judgment will be the best guide. If you find yourself in this kind of situation and you need a few extra moments to analyze the situation and make the best response, you might consider a technique for gaining time that we call "pipe lighting."

Have you ever seen a politician stop to light his pipe before answering a reporter's question? This technique gives one extra time to decide what to say. To gain a little time to think, people do such things as lean back in their chair for a moment, look up at the ceiling, or lightly rub the chin while making verbal encouragements.

The idea behind these activities is to convey that you are thinking during these short pauses in the conversation. But remember, if the time drags on into minutes, the client may perceive your activities as boredom, inattentiveness, or lack of knowledge.

PUTTING IT ALL TOGETHER

As a guide to putting it all together, we have included the following exercises.

Read these examples of client statements. Ask either an open-ended question or a closed-ended question following each statement. Explain why you decided to ask an open-ended or closed-ended question.

EXAMPLE
CLIENT: I've tried everything I can think of. I can't think of anything else to do.
HELPER: What have you tried?

▶ **EXERCISE 1**

CLIENT: I know my teacher hates me. I'm sure that is why I've been getting into so much trouble.

HELPER: _____

▶ **EXERCISE 2**

CLIENT: I can't talk about this anymore today. I think I'd better leave.

HELPER: _____

▶ **EXERCISE 3**

CLIENT: I have a lot of problems. It's hard to know where to start. I guess I'll start with my marriage. This is my second marriage, and we've been married for six years. He drinks alot, and that's part of the problem. I have children from my first marriage, and that's another part of the problem. We also are trying to pay for another child he had in his first marriage, and that's a problem, too.

HELPER: _____

▶ **EXERCISE 4**

CLIENT: I've never been to a counselor before, and I really don't know what to say.

HELPER: _____

Read the following examples of client statements. Ask a closed-ended question following each one to obtain more information about the situation.

▶ **EXERCISE 1**

CLIENT: I'm sorry our time is up. I wish we had more time.

HELPER: _____

▶ **EXERCISE 2**

CLIENT: Now that my shift at work has been changed, I'm going to have a problem getting to work.

HELPER: _____

▶ **EXERCISE 3**

CLIENT: My husband doesn't get along with my son. My son is from a previous marriage, and he is borderline retarded. I don't think my husband handles that very well.

HELPER: _____

(Study Guide begins on page 46.)

STUDY GUIDE

REVIEW QUESTIONS

Make sure you can answer all of the following questions. If you are unable to answer any question, reread that section of the chapter, and try the question again. It will be important that you know this information before beginning the practice sessions.

1. What is the difference between an open-ended question and a closed-ended question?

2. When is it particularly important to ask open-ended questions?

3. When is it particularly important to ask closed-ended questions?

4. There are three activities recommended in making an open-ended question.
   - What are they?
   - What does each activity involve?

5. There are three activities recommended in making a closed-ended question.
   - What are they?
   - What does each activity involve?

6. When might it be appropriate to use a "pipe-lighting" technique?
   - How might you do it?

SKILLS PRACTICE

Here are an example and several exercises in which a student and a partner can practice the skill of questioning. For additional practice, you can create your own situations. Here is an example of how a partner might role play a problem situation to provide practice for this skills:

EXAMPLE

CLIENT (Partner): It's pretty complicated. Seems like everything is going wrong at once.

HELPER (Student): *Should ask open-ended question and pause.*

CLIENT: I just can't afford this apartment anymore, but I also can't seem to afford to move.

HELPER: *Should make verbal encouragements and ask a question.*

CLIENT: I'm already late with my electricity, gas, and phone bills. It gets overwhelming. . . .

HELPER: *Should ask a question or make a reflecting statement.*

▶ ### EXERCISE 1

You have just sat down with the helper, and are waiting for the helper to start the session.

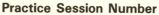

SKILLS CHECKLIST

Skill

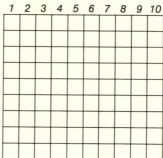

Open-ended questions and pauses
Closed-ended questions and pauses
Reflecting statements and pauses
Active listening
    Posture
    Eye contact
    Facial expression
    Nonverbal encouragements
    Verbal encouragements

Practice Session Number
1 2 3 4 5 6 7 8 9 10

✔ = well done;   o = needs work

► **EXERCISE 2**

You are concerned about your daughter. Her teacher has told you that she works hard but doesn't seem to be able to keep up with the other children. The teacher recommended that she repeat the grade. You have come for advice concerning this situation.

► **EXERCISE 3**

You want your spouse to go to a doctor because he or she has been complaining of stomach pains for over a week. You have been unsuccessful in convincing him or her to go. You are hoping the counselor has some ideas about how to do this.

► **EXERCISE 4**

You are feeling confused about your future, and have come for help in trying to sort through the many different ideas you have.

8

How to Summarize

Effective helpers can guide the counseling relationship by reviewing topics discussed during the session. This is called summarizing. Summarizing helps to recall and link up the topics discussed in the session. This also provides a chance to move on to another topic or to add to what has already been discussed.

When to Use

Summarize in the following situations:

- The helper wants to review the discussion of a specific topic.

- The helper repeats the alternatives identified for solving the client's problem.

- The helper has to end a counseling session.

- The helper is starting a counseling session with a client with whom he or she has met before.

Here are two examples of summarizing statements after the client has said, "That's all I can think of."

- We've thought of lots of different ways you could solve your problem. Let me review them. You could continue looking for a job. You could apply for welfare while looking for a job to help with the money situation. You could talk to the people at the employment agency. You could register at a private employment agency. You could forget looking for a job right now and move in with your mother until you eventually hear about your old job. Did I include everything we've thought of?

- "Let's go over what we've talked about so far. You said that you have been worried about your health. You don't want to go to a doctor, but don't know how else to figure out what is wrong with the way you are feeling. Is that right?"

There are three activities in summarizing:

1. Make a summarizing statement.

2. Ask the client to confirm or dispute the summarizing statement.

3. Listen actively.

1. Make a Summarizing Statement

You should use an appropriate initial phrase and then describe the content of the discussion. This means stating the content or feeling of the client's statements using either the same or different words as were used by the client. New topics should be omitted from this statement.

Some examples of good initial phrases for summarizing statements are:

- "Let's go over what we've talked about so far."
- "Here are the alternatives we've thought of."
- "Let's review this."
- "We talked last time about . . ."

Summarizing statements provide an opportunity for the client to correct any misunderstandings the helper may have about what the client is saying. They also provide an opportunity for either the client or helper to make any additional comments about the topic being discussed.

2. Ask the Client to Confirm or Dispute the Summarizing Statement

You can do this by asking the client a closed-ended question to determine whether the summarizing statement was correct and complete. You should pause, making no verbalizations for at least 5 seconds, following the end of the statement.

Some examples of how you can ask a client to confirm or dispute the summarizing statement are:

- "Is that right?"
- "Has that summarized it?"
- "Did that include everything we've thought of?"

Asking the client to confirm or dispute a summarizing statement encourages the client to correct the helper if he or she is incorrect; pausing indicates that feedback is requested from the client. This makes it more likely that both the helper and client will understand what the other says.

3. Listen Actively

You should maintain eye contact. Keep a straight face, and don't smile. Lean forward while making the summarizing statement. Make a verbal of nonverbal encouragement following the response of the client to your closed-ended question.

Listening actively while summarizing communicates a real interest in helping the client. It shows the client that you are actively involved in helping solve the problem.

Clients will confirm, partially confirm, or reject your summarizing statement. It is important that you be able to determine whether or not the client has confirmed your statement.

To *confirm* your summarizing statement, the client might do or say several things. He or she might nod, or smile, or say something like "right," "yep," or "uh-huh."

To *partially confirm* your summarizing statement, the client might say something like: "I guess...," "kind of...," or "We also talked about...."

To *reject* your summarizing statement, the client might say something like "no" or "not really" or just shake his or her head back and forth.

If It Is Necessary, Ask the Client to Correct the Summarizing Statement

If your summarizing statement is partially confirmed or disputed, you should ask an open-ended question, using an appropriate facial expression and posture. Follow your question with a pause.

Some examples of open-ended questions that can be used to ask a client to correct a summarizing statement are:

- "What else did we talk about?"

- "What have I omitted?"

- "What did I leave out?"

As a guide to putting it all together, we have included the following exercises.

Read the dialogues between a client and helper. Use the skill of summarizing to fill in the blanks in each exercise.

▶ **EXERCISE 1**

HELPER: What are some ways you can think of to lose weight?
CLIENT: Well, I've been ignoring it for a long time, and I guess I could always keep trying to live with being overweight.
HELPER: Uh-huh.
CLIENT: I could talk to a doctor again and this time try to follow through on what he tells me to do.
HELPER: Uh-huh. Have you thought about joining Weight Watchers?
CLIENT: Yeah. I thought about it a long time ago, but never got around to calling them. The Y usually has an exercise class. Maybe that would help.
HELPER: Uh-huh. Can you think of anything else?
CLIENT: No.
HELPER: I can't either.

HELPER: _____

CLIENT: That's a good summary.

HELPER: _____

▶ **EXERCISE 2**

CLIENT: I don't know what kind of work I want to do.
HELPER: Let's try to think of all the possible ways you can solve that problem.
CLIENT: Okay.

HELPER: What different ways can you think of to figure out what kind of work you want to do?

CLIENT: Well, I thought I could get a job and see if I like the kind of work it is. I don't know if that is a good idea because the job market is pretty tight these days. Who knows what kind of a job I could get—maybe doing something I already know I don't want to do.

HELPER: Let's not worry about how good or bad the ideas sound at this point. Let's just think of all the ways we can that will help you make your decision.

CLIENT: Okay. I could also talk to people who are working at different jobs and see how they like their jobs.

HELPER: Uh-huh.

CLIENT: I know a lot of people who do a lot of different things, so maybe that would give me an idea about a lot of different jobs.

HELPER: Uh-huh. Have you thought about going to the library and reading about different occupations?

CLIENT: No, I didn't know the library had that kind of information.

HELPER: Yes, it does.

CLIENT: Well, that's an idea.

HELPER: Have you also thought about talking to a career counselor and finding out what kinds of jobs might be good ones for you?

CLIENT: Nope, hadn't thought of that one either.

HELPER: Can we think of any more ways you can figure out what kind of job to get?

CLIENT: I could go back to school and see what I like there, and get a job in that field.

HELPER: Uh-huh. Any more ideas?

CLIENT: No.

HELPER: I can't think of any more now either.

HELPER: _____

CLIENT: Fine.

HELPER: _____

SUMMARY

In summary, the steps in summarizing a client's comments are as follows:

1. Make a summarizing statement.

2. Ask the client to confirm or dispute the summarizing statement.

3. Listen actively.

If your summarizing statement is partially or completely rejected, ask the client to correct the summarizing statement.

(Study Guide begins on page 52.)

STUDY GUIDE

REVIEW QUESTIONS

Make sure you can answer all of the following questions. If you are unable to answer any question, reread that section of the chapter, and try the question again. It will be important that you know this information before beginning the practice session.

1. When is it particularly important to summarize?

2. There are three activities recommended in summarizing a client's concerns.

   • What are they?

   • What does each activity involve?

3. Why is summarizing an important counseling skill?

4. What is the counselor to do if the client partially or completely rejects the summary?

   • What does this involve?

SKILLS PRACTICE

Here are an example and several exercises in which a student and a partner can practice the skill of summarizing. For additional practice, you can create your own situations. Here is an example of how a partner might role play a problem situation to provide practice for this skill:

EXAMPLE

CLIENT (Partner): "I've been killing myself trying to be a good parent since my wife died..." (*Pauses*)

HELPER (Student): *Should make verbal encouragements like "Uh-huh."*

CLIENT: The three boys seem happy enough, but I'm concerned that my daughter doesn't have her mother to talk to anymore... (*Pauses*)

HELPER: *Should make verbal encouragements like "I see."*

CLIENT: I don't know what to do. Maybe Sarah's teacher would talk to her now that she's getting to be a teenager. I don't know. Maybe I will ask her to talk with Sarah. I think I'll go down to the school tomorrow after I get off work..." (*Long pause*)

HELPER: Seems like you're really not sure which way to turn.

CLIENT: I'm not. I have so many thoughts going on in my mind. It gets confusing.

HELPER: *Should make a summarizing statement, ask the client to confirm or dispute it, and listen actively.*

▶ ### EXERCISE 1

You are a client who is very worried over the possibility of losing your job. Your employer has announced that he or she will be laying people off, and you wanted to talk to somebody about what you should do.

SKILLS CHECKLIST

Skill

Practice Session Number

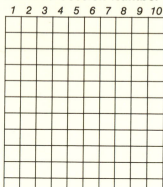

Summarizing statement
Ask to confirm or dispute
Active listening
    Posture
    Eye contact
    Facial expression
    Nonverbal encouragements
    Verbal encouragements
Reflecting statements and pauses
Open-ended questions and pauses
Closed-ended questions and pauses

✔ = well done;   o = needs work

► **EXERCISE 2**

You've seen this helper before, but you have a new problem now. You don't like the friends of your adolescent son. You think they are a bad influence on your son. You have come for ideas about what to do about this situation.

► **EXERCISE 3**

You are a client who strongly dislikes one of your high school teachers. You would like to change teachers, but don't know how to do it.

► **EXERCISE 4**

Your spouse has been very depressed recently, and this has been very upsetting to you. You are worried about him or her, and have come for help with this situation.

9

Introduction to the Problem-Solving Index

The purpose of this chapter is to provide background information that you will use in helping counsel people with problems. Part III of this book contains a wealth of information about everyday client problems. There are numerous alternatives suggested to solve these problems. Also included is an analysis of the various consequences that may follow the selection of any solution. For your convenience, this information is organized in an index containing literally hundreds of problem-solving ideas.

The Index is divided into two sections. The first section lists 254 specific problems for which clients come to counselors. They are categorized under the headings of Education Problems, Family and Friends Problems, Financial Problems, Health Problems, Housing Problems, Occupation Problems, and Self-Improvement Problems. For example, under the heading of Education Problems, you will find listed such situations as a child who is thinking about quitting school and a young woman who is thinking about learning a trade.

Each specific problem is followed by a list of possible alternative solutions. For example, the problem of an unhappy marriage is followed by a list of such possible alternative solutions as seeking professional marital counseling, trying a marital separation, obtaining a divorce, or talking to a clergy member.

Each possible alternative solution to the problems listed in the first section of the Index is followed by a number. This number refers you to the appropriate item in the second section, which lists possible consequences, both good and bad, that might occur were the client to select the alternative. In the situation of a client with an unhappy marriage, some possible consequences of divorce as an alternative include financial problems, child stress or benefit, or possible increased happiness for the partners. In all, the Index, with 254 problem situations and 176 alternative solutions, is an extraordinary resource for the student interested in expanding options available to his or her clients.

The following exercises are designed to help you become familiar with the Index and its many uses.

 EXERCISE 1
Using the Problem-Solving Index in Part III of this book, list five specific problems in each major problem category:

A. EDUCATION

1. _____
2. _____
3. _____
4. _____
5. _____

B. FAMILY AND FRIENDS

1. _____
2. _____
3. _____
4. _____
5. _____

C. FINANCIAL

1. _____
2. _____
3. _____
4. _____
5. _____

D. HEALTH

1. _____
2. _____
3. _____
4. _____
5. _____

E. HOUSING

1. _____
2. _____
3. _____
4. _____
5. _____

(Exercise 1 continues on page 56.)

F. OCCUPATION

1. _____

2. _____

3. _____

4. _____

5. _____

G. SELF-IMPROVEMENT

1. _____

2. _____

3. _____

4. _____

5. _____

▶ **EXERCISE 2**

Using the Index, list all of the alternatives for at least one specific problem in each of the major problem categories. Try to think of other alternatives not listed in the Index.

A. EDUCATION

Specific Problem: _____

Alternatives: _____

_____

_____

_____

_____

_____

B. FAMILY AND FRIENDS

Specific Problem: _____

Alternatives: _____

_____

_____

_____

_____

_____

C. FINANCIAL

Specific Problem: _____

Alternatives: _____

_____

_____

_____

_____

_____

D. HEALTH

Specific Problem: _____

Alternatives: _____

_____

_____

_____

_____

_____

E. HOUSING

Specific Problem: _____

Alternatives: _____

_____

_____

_____

_____

_____

F. OCCUPATION

Specific Problem: _____

Alternatives: _____

_____

_____

_____

_____

_____

(Exercise 2 continues on page 58.)

G. SELF-IMPROVEMENT

Specific Problem: _____

Alternatives: _____

_____

_____

_____

_____

_____

▶ **EXERCISE 3**

Using the Index, list all the consequences for each of at least five different alternatives. (*Note:* The number to the right of each alternative solution is the same number as on top of the list of possible consequences found in the second part of the Index. Try to think of other consequences not listed in the Index.)

1. **Specific Problem:** _____

   Alternative: _____

   Consequences: _____

   _____

   _____

   _____

   _____

2. **Specific Problem:** _____

   Alternative: _____

   Consequences: _____

   _____

   _____

   _____

   _____

3. **Specific Problem:** _____

   Alternative: _____

   Consequences: _____

   _____

   _____

   _____

   _____

4. **Specific Problem:** _____

   Alternative: _____

   Consequences: _____

   _____

   _____

   _____

   _____

5. **Specific Problem:** _____

   Alternative: _____

   Consequences: _____

   _____

   _____

   _____

   _____

Spend some time familiarizing yourself with the problems, alternative solutions, and consequences listed in the Index. Knowledge of the included information can add greatly to your ability to counsel people.

As a means of putting it all together, we have included the following exercises. Read each example of a client's problem. For each one, determine under which major heading the problem is located, write down all alternatives listed, as well as any others you can think of, and analyze the possible consequences for each alternative solution.

(Exercises are on page 60.)

▶ **EXERCISE 1**

CLIENT: My wife is becoming an alcoholic. She's drinking much too much, but doesn't think she has a problem. I know she needs help, but I don't know what to do about it.

Problem Heading: _____

Alternatives/Consequences: _____

_____

_____

_____

_____

_____

▶ **EXERCISE 2**

CLIENT: I need help finding a job.

Problem Heading: _____

Alternatives/Consequences: _____

_____

_____

_____

_____

_____

▶ **EXERCISE 3**

CLIENT: My Welfare check just doesn't cover all my expenses. I can't even buy my poor baby new shoes to start school with because they don't give us any clothing allowance. I know I can't get more money from Welfare, but I have got to do something. I can't live on what I receive each month.

Problem Heading: _____

Alternatives/Consequences: _____

_____

_____

_____

_____

_____

10

How to Help a Client Solve a Problem

Clients and friends come to a helper because they are having a problem. Sometimes they simply need to talk about the problem situation. In these cases, the counselor's responsibility is to be a good listener and help the client ventilate his or her feelings. The skills of listening actively, reflecting feelings, and open-ended question-asking will be very effective in helping a person do this.

At other times, people need help solving a problem. In these cases, the counselor's responsibility is to help the client understand the problem situation, think of alternative solutions, evaluate each, and select the best one.

This chapter is designed to teach problem-solving skills that enable helpers to assist clients in reaching satisfactory decisions. It is important that the counselor *assist* the client in solving problems, not solve problems *for* the client. By demonstrating a systematic problem-solving approach, the helper provides an example of how the client might solve his or her problems in the future.

Address the client by name throughout the problem-solving process. This helps to encourage the client to be honest and open.

When to Use

Use the systematic problem-solving approach in the following situations:

• The client requests help in solving a problem.

• The client requests help in choosing solutions to a problem.

• The client requests help in taking action on a selected plan.

Here is an example of a counselor helping a client solve a problem.

HELPER: What seems to be the problem, Kay?
CLIENT: My son has no friends in school.
HELPER: Uh-huh.
CLIENT: I tried talking to his teacher about it, but that didn't do any good. (*Sighs and pauses*)
HELPER: You sound very depressed about the whole thing.
CLIENT: I am.
HELPER: Could you tell me more about it?
CLIENT: Sure. He's in the fourth grade, and has no friends. He's very quiet anyway,

but I understand he says very little in school. At home he has his sister and brothers to play with, but I'm worried because he is always by himself at school.

HELPER: Uh-huh.

CLIENT: I don't know if it has gotten worse or anything. I just think he's getting to the age where he needs to have friends his own age. I mean, other children all play with children their own age, don't they?

HELPER: Sounds like you're worried that the problem might get worse if you don't do something about it soon.

CLIENT: Right. I probably should have done something about it a long time ago.

HELPER: It seems like you have some feelings about that.

CLIENT: I do, but that gets into a whole different story.

HELPER: Would you like to talk about it?

CLIENT: Someday, but not now.

HELPER: So the problem seems to be that your son doesn't have any friends his own age. Is that right?

CLIENT: Yes.

HELPER: Kay, let's look at all the ways we can think of to help you get your son more involved with children his own age. Most people find it useful to think of as many alternatives as they can before making a decision.

CLIENT: Okay.

HELPER: What ideas do you have? I'm going to write them all down so we don't forget any.

CLIENT: Okay. I've been thinking about going in and talking to his teacher again. I've talked to him once, but it was a long time ago. It didn't do any good then, but it might be better if I talked with him again.

HELPER: That's an idea.

CLIENT: I've already tried talking to my son about it, but he doesn't want to talk about it at all.

HELPER: So, Kay, another alternative might be trying to talk to him again?

CLIENT: Anything is worth a try at this point.

HELPER: Can you think of any other things you can do?

CLIENT: Um . . .

HELPER: Have you thought about your husband, son, and yourself talking to a professional counselor about the problem?

CLIENT: No. That might be a good idea. I hadn't thought of that.

HELPER: Let's see. What else could you do?

CLIENT: I could always just keep waiting and hoping it's only a phase. That's really what I've been doing, you know.

HELPER: Uh-huh. Can you think of any other things to do?

CLIENT: No.

HELPER: (*Pauses*) Let me think. (*Pauses*) I can't either. Kay, let me read back the alternatives we've thought of. You could try talking to your son's teacher again. You could talk to your son. We thought of your husband, son, and you talking to a professional counselor. We also thought of just waiting and hoping the problem passes with time. Can you think of any more?

CLIENT: No. The list sounds pretty complete.

HELPER: How about talking with the school psychologist? She might have experience with this kind of problem. I'll add it to the list. Kay, let's look at each one and think about what might happen if you were to do it. What do you think would happen if you talked to your son's teacher again?

CLIENT: Probably nothing.

HELPER: I see.

CLIENT: He's pretty strict with his students, and doesn't have much sympathy for children who are having problems. Last time I talked to him, he said children's problems are all caused by their parents. Maybe that's true, but it didn't help me out at all.

HELPER: I can understand that.

CLIENT: Anyway, I don't expect it to help, but maybe talking to him again would be worth a try.

HELPER: One thing that might come out of it is letting him know you are really concerned about your son. That might make him listen to you more.

CLIENT: Never thought of that. Could be, but with him, I don't know.

HELPER: So, Kay, how would you rate this idea? Excellent? Fair? Poor?

CLIENT: Oh, I'd say fair.

HELPER: Okay. What about talking to your son? How does that alternative sound?

CLIENT: That's the worst on the list. Believe me, I've tried. He won't talk, gets very angry when I bring the subject up, and we usually end up yelling at each other, which defeats the whole purpose.

HELPER: Doesn't sound like you feel that's a promising avenue to take.

CLIENT: No, I don't.

HELPER: How would you rate it, excellent, fair, or poor?

CLIENT: Oh, rate that one as poor.

HELPER: What might happen if you all went to a professional counselor for help?

CLIENT: I think it would do us all good.

HELPER: I see.

CLIENT: I know it would do me good.

HELPER: Uh-huh.

CLIENT: I like that idea.

HELPER: What are you imagining would come from it?

CLIENT: Well, we could get everything out in the open. My son won't talk to me, but maybe he'd talk to a counselor about what's been going on with him.

HELPER: Uh-huh. You sound more positive about this idea.

CLIENT: I am.

HELPER: Professional counseling may cost you something.

CLIENT: It would be well worth it if it helped.

HELPER: Are there any other outcomes you can think of?

CLIENT: No.

HELPER: How would you rate this idea?

CLIENT: Excellent.

HELPER: What about talking to the school psychologist?

CLIENT: Not as good. It could help, but then again, if my son found out, he'd be mad because he's told me to leave him alone about it.

HELPER: What are your feelings about that, Kay?

CLIENT: Well, he doesn't talk that often, so when he says something, I try to respect it. I'd hate to embarrass him in front of his peers. That could end up making him even more withdrawn and alone. You know how kids are.

HELPER: Yeah, I do. One possible advantage, though, is that you might get some ideas from the school psychologist because she may have been able to observe your son in school.

CLIENT: I know. It might help, but I'd rather get professional help outside of the school.

HELPER: I keep noticing that you favor the professional counselor.

CLIENT: I am, and there's another reason, too. My husband and I are in disagreement about what to do about our son. I think we could use the help of a counselor ourselves.

HELPER: You sound pretty positive about things working out alright.

CLIENT: Talking about them now is making me realize that I really am. I think my husband and I need to get some things squared away between ourselves, and I know that we'll be able to do that.

HELPER: Where would you rate the school psychologist idea?

CLIENT: Between excellent and fair.

HELPER: We also listed just waiting. How do you feel about that alternative?

CLIENT: It's out of the question. I can't afford to wait anymore.

HELPER: Here's the list, Kay, and the way you rated each alternative. Which one sounds the best?

CLIENT: The professional counselor. I like that idea, and I think it's going to help.

HELPER: Sounds good, huh?

CLIENT: Yes.

HELPER: Sounds good to me, too. Do you have any further questions about how to find a counselor?

CLIENT: No. I'm sure my friends can recommend someone.

HELPER: Please let me know how things work out.

CLIENT: I will. This has been so helpful. Thank you.

We recommend a series of activities to help a client solve a problem. Each is described below; all fourteen are listed in the summary at the end of this chapter.

Request a Problem Statement

You should request a problem statement by asking an open-ended question. The question should be followed by a pause of at least five seconds.

It is sometimes the case that the client will state the problem without the counselor's requesting a problem statement. Some clients begin speaking about their problems without any specific request from the counselor. If this occurs, go to the next step, which is to define the problem.

Define the Problem

You should repeat the problem statement either in your own words or in the client's. Use a closed-ended question to make sure of your understanding of the problem. Wait in silence for the client to confirm or dispute your definition of the problem. If the client partially confirms or disputes your definition of the problem, ask the client for another problem statement, and attempt once again to define the problem. When the client confirms your definition, you may want to write the problem down on a sheet of paper.

Figure 3. Headings for a Problem-Solving Worksheet

Client's Name: _____

Date: _____

Counselor's Name: _____

Problem: _____

Alternatives: _____

Waiting for a confirmation is a way to make sure you and the client are talking about the same thing. It also gives your client an opportunity to add or clarify something so that you can have a fuller picture of the problem situation.

Writing the problem down can serve several purposes. For one, it will allow you to list all the alternatives suggested during the problem-solving process. This will help you remember all the alternatives mentioned and will help you sum up when closing the helping session. It will also be useful if the client requests further help. The written information will refresh your memory of an earlier meeting with the client.

Use two sheets of paper with carbon paper between them. This way you can file one copy for yourself and you can give one copy to the client. One way to set up the paper is in a problem-solving worksheet (see Figure 3).

Here are two ways to request a problem statement and define the problem:

EXAMPLE 1

HELPER: What seems to be the problem?

CLIENT: I'm totally out of money because I haven't been able to find a job in the past five months.

HELPER: So it seems the problem is that you need a job soon or some money to hold you over until you can find one. Is that right?

CLIENT: Yep, that's it.

EXAMPLE 2

HELPER: How would you describe the problem?

CLIENT: My father is getting pretty old. He forgets things and is barely able to take care of himself anymore. He is living by himself, and that worries me. I don't know what to do.

HELPER: Let me make sure I'm clear. The problem is that your father is getting old and can't take care of himself anymore. Is that correct?

CLIENT: Yes, and I don't think he can come live with me.

Here is one way to request a problem statement and define the problem after a client rejects the helper's problem statement. Notice how the helper attempts to define the problem again:

EXAMPLE

HELPER: What seems to be the problem?

CLIENT: I'm totally out of money because I haven't been able to find a job in the past five months.

HELPER: I imagine that must be creating a problem between you and your wife.

CLIENT: No, my wife is very understanding.

HELPER: What is the problem then?

CLIENT: I'm getting very depressed from having nothing to do. I need to find a job.

HELPER: So, you're needing some help in finding a job, is that right?

CLIENT: Yeah, that's right.

The outcome is a list of one or more problem statements. Write only one statement per sheet of paper. Clients may need help with more than one problem. We recommend that you assist a client in solving one problem at a time.

Explain the Problem-Solving Process

You should explain to the client how you will be helping to solve his or her problem. Provide a rationale for using this process. You might include saying that you and the client will be thinking of possible ways to solve the problem. You might want to encourage the client to tell you any alternatives he or she thinks of, regardless of how they may sound at first. It can be helpful to tell the client that by looking at the possible positive and negative outcomes of each alternative, he or she should be able to make the best decision. You may also want to explain why you are writing down the alternatives mentioned.

State the Usefulness of the Problem-Solving Process

After explaining the problem-solving process, you should tell the client that the process will be useful. You might also want to say that upon completion of the problem-solving process, the client may be able to make future decisions on his or her own using this systematic process.

Examples of how to explain the problem-solving process and its usefulness to a client are:

• "We're going to figure out as many ways of solving your problem as we can. The best way to make a good decision is to look at each possible solution and figure out its consequences. Let's think of all the solutions we can, regardless of whether they sound good or bad. I'm going to write everything down so we don't forget any of them. It should be a very useful process for helping you solve your problem."

• "We're going to use a systematic approach to problem solving. It involves thinking of all possible alternatives for solving your problem, regardless of how good or bad they sound. I'll write them down. We'll look at the pros and cons of each, and you should be able to decide on a way to solve your problem. By going through this process with me, it may make it easier to solve a future problem on your own."

An explanation of the problem-solving process will give a client an overview of what will follow. It can help make a client feel more relaxed. It also can make the problem-solving process go faster because a client knows beforehand what you will do and what will be expected.

Stating the usefulness of the problem-solving process can give encouragement to a client who may feel that there is no solution to his or her problem.

 ## Identify Alternative Solutions

To identify alternative solutions, first ask a client to tell you all the possible solutions he or she can think of to the problem. Write these down. No possible solutions should be excluded. Second, ask open-ended questions to encourage the client to consider any solutions that you suggest. You may want to use the Problem-Solving Index in Part III of this book for additional ideas.

You might introduce your ideas with open-ended phrases, such as, "Have you thought about...?" or "What about...?" It is best *not* to suggest your alternatives by saying, "You should do...," or "You ought to...." Effective helpers neither argue for their own suggestions nor evaluate negatively or positively those of the client. Take special care not to play with you pen during the helping session, lest you seem bored or impatient. Also, take care not to talk as you write, because it is difficult to concentrate on either when you do both together.

Examples of how to introduce this method are:

- "Let's see what alternatives we can think of. What ideas do you have?"
- "Let's list all the possibilities to solving the problem that we can. What are some you can think of?"

One cannot, at this point, determine which alternative will turn out to be the best for the client. You must encourage the client to mention *any* idea at all, regardless of how unlikely it may sound. This is the time to think of as many solutions as possible. Sometimes the most farfetched ideas turn out to be the best. A client will often feel much better knowing that many possible solutions exist.

Don't make negative or positive evaluations of any alternative at this point. Your neutrality may encourage the client to feel freer to voice any idea. In reality, a counselor does not know the consequences an alternative may have in a client's life. If you were to offer your opinion of an alternative at this point, a client might begin to feel that you are pushing your ideas without fully understanding his or her situation.

Write down all the alternatives that both of you mention. Figure 4 is an example of a partially completed problem-solving worksheet.

To help put together what you have learned so far, we have included the following exercises. Read these examples of client problems. Define the problem, explain the problem-solving process, state its usefulness, and write down as many possible solutions as you can. You may want to use the Problem-Solving Index in Part III to help you identify alternative solutions. Keep your lists because you will be using them again in another exercise later in this chapter.

(Exercises begin on page 68.)

Figure 4. Partially Completed Problem-Solving Worksheet

Client's Name: Susan Singer

Date: February 26, 1980

Counselor's Name: Kathy Langer

Problem: Gets lonely

Alternatives:

1. Join club in school to meet new people

2. Join church youth group to meet new people

3. Talk to new person in class

4. Talk to professional counselor

5. Join sports team

6. Find satisfying hobby you can do by yourself

7. Make plans to do things with friends

8. Do things with your family

▶ **EXERCISE 1**

CLIENT: I need some help in making a decision. I just graduated from high school, and I've been trying to decide if I should go to vocational school or start apprenticing as a carpenter. The money would be good if I worked, but maybe it would be better to keep going to school. What do you think?

Problem: _____

Explanation of problem-solving process: _____

_____

State its usefulness: _____

Alternatives: _____

_____

_____

_____

_____

_____

▶ **EXERCISE 2**

CLIENT: School's going to be starting soon, and I don't even have money to buy my children new school shoes. Welfare makes no clothing allowance at all, and it's getting so that I can't make things come out even anymore.

Problem: _____

Explanation of problem-solving process: _____

_____

State its usefulness: _____

Alternatives: _____

_____

_____

_____

_____

_____

EXERCISE 3

CLIENT: I've been feeling so nervous lately. It's not about anything special. I thought I should do something about it, and I didn't know who else to talk to about it.

Problem: _____

Explanation of problem-solving process: _____

_____

State its usefulness: _____

Alternatives: _____

_____

_____

_____

_____

_____

(Chapter 10 continues on page 70.)

Summarize the Alternatives Mentioned

You should make a summarizing statement. Include all the alternatives you and the client have mentioned. You can do this by reading the list of alternatives you have written down. Remember to ask the client if there are any other alternatives not yet mentioned.

Here is an example of a counselor summarizing the alternatives identified:

- "Let's go over the alternatives we've thought of. You can join clubs in school or join your church youth group to meet new people, talk to a new person in class, talk to a professional counselor for more help, join a sports team, find a hobby you'd like to do by yourself, make plans to do things with friends, or do things with your family. Can you think of any more?"

As with all summarizing statements, summarizing the alternatives identified provides an opportunity for the client or helper to make additional comments. It signals the client that you both are ready to move on to the next phase of the process.

Turn the Worksheet toward the Client

Turn the paper on which the alternatives are listed toward the client so that he or she may easily read through the list. You might want to ask if there are any other solutions that should be added to the list.

People often find it useful to read the list because it makes it easier to remember the alternatives mentioned. Sharing the list with the client can help the client remain active in the problem-solving process. Remember good counselors *help* a client solve a problem; they don't *solve* the problem for a client.

Analyze the Possible Consequences of Each Alternative

You should introduce the next phase of the problem-solving process by telling the client that analyzing the consequences of each alternative will help him or her make the best decision. Ask the client to state all possible outcomes for each listed alternative. You should also state any consequence you can think of, even if it probably doesn't apply to the client's situation. You may want to use the Index in Part III for additional ideas. No consequence should be excluded.

The analysis of possible consequences should include a consideration of the following things:

1. benefits gained for the client and others,
2. problems caused for the client and others,
3. feelings that could be aroused for the client and others,
4. availability of the alternative,
5. any entrance requirements; that is, conditions that may have to precede the alternative.

It can be helpful to ask the client a specific question about each of these five considerations for each alternative before considering the next one.

Some examples of how to ask a client to consider the consequences of each alternative are as follows:

- "What do you think would happen if you choose this one?"
- "What outcomes would be likely if you decided to do this?"
- "How do you feel about this idea?"
- "What are the advantages of this one? What are the disadvantages?"

Since the consequences of any solution affect the client's level of satisfaction, the careful analysis of each alternative is an important aspect of problem solving.

Note: Clients often express many feelings (both verbally and nonverbally) while analyzing the positive and negative consequences of each alternative. Try to make reflecting statements when you observe these feelings.

Here is an example of a client and helper analyzing the consequences of one alternative. Note how the helper reflects the client's feelings. Also note the open-ended style that introduces the consequences the helper mentions.

HELPER: Let's look at the advantages and disadvantages of each alternative. That should help you make the best decision about what to do. The first one is going back to school. How do you think you might benefit from doing that?

CLIENT: Well, I could probably get a better job after I finish.

HELPER: Uh-huh. What other advantages might there be?

CLIENT: I know I would enjoy being back in school.

HELPER: You sound like that's an exciting thought.

CLIENT: It is. I've often thought about wanting to return to school. I liked being in school.

HELPER: What other benefits might there be?

CLIENT: Just mostly being able to get a better job.

HELPER: Have you thought about the fact that going back to school may give you a way to meet a whole new group of people?

CLIENT: That's true. I think that's partly why I've been wanting to go back to school.

HELPER: Can you think of any more benefits of going back to school?

CLIENT: No.

HELPER: I can't either. What problems might be caused by it?

CLIENT: The main one is that I'll have to find some way to support myself if I give up my job to go back to school.

HELPER: Yep. What other disadvantages might there be?

CLIENT: Well, what happens if I've forgotten how to study?

HELPER: You seem to be concerned about that.

CLIENT: I am. It's probably why I've never enrolled in school again.

HELPER: *(Makes nonverbal encouragements)*

CLIENT: I've had many people tell me not to worry about it, but I guess I do.

HELPER: It sounds like it's the main reason you have for not going back to school.

CLIENT: I guess it's really the only reason.

HELPER: Are there other disadvantages to going back to school except perhaps having difficulty with the studying?

CLIENT: Not really.

HELPER: Have you considered whether or not you can get into the program?

CLIENT: Ah, thanks for reminding me about that. I'd really like to return to school,

and sometimes I forget that I still have to be accepted.
HELPER: (*Nods head*) What else do you think might happen if you go back to school?
CLIENT: Really, nothing bad.
HELPER: I can't think of anything else.

Carefully analyzing each alternative in this way will help a client choose the best plan of action. Questioning a client about the advantages, disadvantages, availability, and any entrance requirements helps to ensure that a chosen alternative is *feasible* and *satisfactory*. Making comments or asking questions about a client's feelings toward an alternative helps to bring into the open any concerns he or she may have toward a possible course of action. You will then be in a better position to help the client deal with his or her concerns.

Return to the list of possible solutions that you identified for the exercises on pages 68 and 69. Think of as many negative and positive consequences for each alternative as you can. You may want to use the Problem-Solving Index in Part III, but also try to think up some others on your own.

Rate Each Alternative

After analyzing the consequences of one alternative, ask a question to determine how satisfactory the client finds that alternative. Use a rating scale, such as excellent, fair, or poor, and write down the client's rating next to each alternative.

Two examples of how to ask a client to rate his or her satisfaction with an alternative are as follows:

- "If you were to label this alternative, what would you call it: excellent, fair, or poor?"

- "How good does this alternative sound? Would you rate it excellent, fair, or poor?"

Writing the rating next to the alternative on the counselor's list will allow a client and counselor to look at the list and see how each alternative is rated in comparison with the others. This will make it easier for a client to see which alternatives he or she favors.

Figure 5 is an example of how a counselor might write a client's ratings of each alternative.

Select the Best Alternative

After every alternative is analyzed and rated, give the list of rated alternatives to the client. Ask the client to select the best alternative or alternatives on the basis of the ratings and your discussion.

An example of asking the client to select the best alternative or alternatives is as follows:

- "Here is the list of alternatives. Based on your ratings and all we've talked about, which ones sound best?"

Figure 5. Completed Problem-Solving Worksheet

Client's Name: Susan Singer

Date: February 26, 1980

Counselor's Name: Kathy Langer

Problem: Gets lonely

Alternatives:	Excellent	Fair	Poor
1. Join club in school to meet new people	X		
2. Join church youth group to meet new people		X	
3. Talk to new person in class	X		
4. Talk to professional counselor		X	
5. Join sports team			X
6. Find satisfying hobby you can do by yourself		X	
7. Make plans to do things with friends	X		
8. Do things with your family			X

Determine Client's Satisfaction with Choice

You should ask an open-ended question to determine if the client is satisfied with his or her selected alternative(s).

If the Client Is Satisfied with the Choice, State Your Support for the Decision

You should tell the client you think the decision is a good one.

Ask if Help Is Needed to Take Action

You should ask a closed-ended question to determine if the client knows how to carry out the chosen alternative(s).

When the client has said he or she is satisfied with the choice, you may follow this example of stating your support for the decision and of asking if help is needed to take action:

- "Carol, you decided that a trial separation from your husband would be the best idea. That sounds like a good idea to me, too. Do you have any questions about how to arrange for the separation?"

(Chapter 10 continues on page 74.)

If It Is Needed, Provide Help in Taking Action

This can be done by suggesting ways of taking action. Ask the client if he or she can think of any others. You may want to write the suggestions down. Make a summarizing statement of the ideas mentioned, and ask a closed-ended question to determine the client's satisfaction with the choice.

Here is an example of asking if help is needed in taking action and in providing that help:

HELPER: Carol, you decided that a trial separation from your husband would be the best idea. That sounds like a good idea to me, too. Do you have any questions about how to arrange it?

CLIENT: Yes. How do I go about doing it?

HELPER: Let's see what ways we can think of. How about calling your family lawyer and finding out what legal issues are involved?

CLIENT: That's a good idea. I think I'll call my friend and use her lawyer, though.

HELPER: What other concerns do you have?

CLIENT: I guess I have to think about where I will live?

HELPER: Do you need help finding a place to live?

CLIENT: Gee, thanks. I think I can take care of that.

HELPER: Are there other things you need help with?

CLIENT: I don't think so at this time.

HELPER: So, it sounds like you think that calling a lawyer is the next thing to do, and then you will think about where to live. Anything else?

CLIENT: No. That's enough.

If the Client Is Not Satisfied with the Choice, Try to Identify More Alternatives

You can do this by asking the client if he or she can make any other suggestions. Analyze the consequences of each of these new alternatives, and ask the client to rate each one.

Select the Best Alternative

Give the complete list of rated alternatives to the client, and ask him or her to select the best one.

When the client chooses an alternative, the counselor should then ask if help is needed to take action and, if it is, provide help.

Note: There may be times when a client chooses an alternative solution that is incompatible with the values of the helper, for example, using violence or illegal or immoral acts to solve a problem. If this occurs, you need not state support for the client's decision nor provide help in taking action. If the client does threaten to do something illegal, you should consult your supervisor or, if you have no supervisor, a municipal agency head or the police.

The problem-solving process outlined above is followed for one problem at a time. If a client has identified more than one problem, repeat all of these activities for each problem.

SUMMARY

In summary, the steps in problem-solving are as follows:

1. Request a problem statement.
2. Define the problem.
3. Explain the problem-solving process.
4. State the usefulness of the problem-solving process.
5. Identify alternative solutions.
6. Summarize the alternatives identified.
7. Turn the list over to the client.
8. Analyze the possible consequences for each alternative.
9. Rate each alternative.
10. Select the best alternative.
11. Determine client's satisfaction with choice.

If the client is satisfied with the choice:

12. State your support for the decision.
13. Ask if help is needed to take action.
14. Provide help in taking action if needed.

If the client is not satisfied with the choice:

12. Try to identify more alternatives.
13. Select the best alternative.
14. Ask if help is needed to take action.
15. Provide help in taking action if needed.

STUDY GUIDE

REVIEW QUESTIONS

Make sure you can answer all of the following questions. If you are unable to answer any question, reread that section of the chapter, and try the question again. It will be important that you know this information before beginning the practice sessions.

1. When is it particularly important to help a client solve a problem?
2. The first activity in problem solving is to request a problem statement. What does this involve?
3. The second activity in problem solving is to define the problem. What does this involve?
4. What does a counselor do if the client partially confirms or disputes his or her definition of the problem?

5. What is the next activity in problem solving?

   • What does it involve?

6. The fourth activity in problem solving is to state the usefulness of the problem-solving process. What does this involve?

7. What do you do after stating the usefulness of the problem-solving process?

   • What does this involve?

8. When identifying alternatives available to the client, it is important that the counselor make no negative or positive judgments of any alternative.

   • Why is this so important?

9. What does the counselor do once all the alternatives have been identified?

10. If no more alternatives can be thought of by either the client or counselor, what is the counselor to do next in the problem-solving process?

    • What does this involve?

11. Especially during the stage of analyzing the consequences of each alternative solution, a counseling skill learned earlier can be important. What is this skill?

12. What is the activity in problem solving after all the consequences of one alternative have been analyzed?

    • What does it involve?

13. After all the alternatives have been analyzed, what does the counselor do next?

    • What does this involve?

14. After the client chooses the best alternative, what should the counselor do next?

    • What does this involve?

15. Why is it a good idea for a counselor to state his support for the client's decision?

16. If the client is satisfied with the choice made in the problem-solving process, what is the thing the counselor should ask the client?

    • What does this involve?

17. If the client says he or she needs help in taking action, the counselor should provide help. What does this involve?

18. What would your problem-solving worksheet look like for a client who has identified alternatives to a problem involving failing grades in school?

SKILLS PRACTiCE

Here are an example and several exercises in which a student and a partner can practice the skills of problem solving. For additional practice, you can create your own situations. Here is an example of how a partner might role play a problem situation to provide practice for this skill:

EXAMPLE

HELPER (Student): *Should request a problem statement.*

CLIENT (Partner): I've been divorced for about six months now, and I feel like my six-year-old daughter is really having some emotional problems because of the divorce. She's not doing as well in school as she was, and I'm very concerned.

HELPER: *Should define the problem.*

CLIENT: That's right.

HELPER: *Should explain the problem-solving process.*

CLIENT: Fine.

HELPER: *Should state the usefulness of the problem-solving process.*

CLIENT: I'm willing to try anything.

HELPER: *Should identify alternative solutions.*

CLIENT: The only thing I can think of is talking to my ex-husband about it.

HELPER: *Should identify alternative solutions.*

CLIENT: That's a good idea. Maybe that one will help.

HELPER: *Should ask client for more alternatives.*

CLIENT: Well, I guess I could just hope the whole thing passes with time.

HELPER: *Should identify alternative solutions.*

HELPER: *Should ask the client for additional solutions.*

CLIENT: I can't think of any more.

HELPER: *Should summarize the alternatives identified.*

CLIENT: I'm amazed. That's quite a list.

HELPER: *Should turn the list to the client.*

CLIENT: Let's see.

HELPER: *Should:*

- *analyze the possible consequences for each alternative,*
- *be listening actively and making reflecting statements,*
- *ask the client to rate each alternative,*
- *ask the client to select the best alternative.*

CLIENT: I like the idea of helping her get involved in new activities and friendships to fill in the gap she must feel. That sounds like exactly the right thing to do.

HELPER: *Should determine the client's satisfaction with the choice.*

CLIENT: I'm very pleased with it.

HELPER: *Should state his or her support of the decision.*

CLIENT: Thank you.

HELPER: *Should ask if help is needed to take action.*

CLIENT: I don't think so.

▶ **EXERCISE 1**

You have a 14-year-old daughter who, you feel, has been acting as though she were 21. You think her friends are too old for her, and are afraid she is heading for trouble. You and your spouse feel you have no control over her. You are hoping the counselor will be able to help you.

▶ **EXERCISE 2**

You have been having trouble sleeping recently. The lack of sleep has begun to interfere with your work performance, and this is upsetting you. You want to talk to somebody to get ideas about what to do.

SKILLS CHECKLIST

Skill

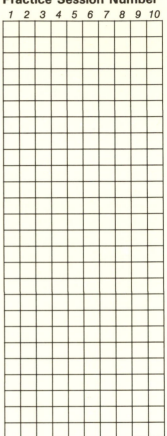

Practice Session Number

	1	2	3	4	5	6	7	8	9	10

Request problem statement
Define problem
Explain problem-solving process
State usefulness of process
Identify alternatives
    Ask client first
    Introduce yours in open-ended manner
Summarize alternatives
Turn list to client
Analyze consequences of each alternative
Rate each alternative
Select best alternative
Determine client satisfaction with choice
Identify other alternatives if not satisfied
State support of decision
Ask if help is needed to take action
Provide help (if needed)
Reflecting statements and pauses
Open-ended questions and pauses
Closed-ended questions and pauses
Active listening
    Posture
    Eye contact
    Facial expression
    Nonverbal encouragements
    Verbal encouragements

✔ = well done;   o = needs work

► **EXERCISE 3**

You can't decide what to do about your parents' interference in your personal life. You are an adult, and don't feel you need them to suggest to you what they think you should do, but you also don't want to hurt their feelings.

► **EXERCISE 4**

You are overweight, which makes you unhappy. You are hoping the counselor will be able to help you learn to lose weight.

11

How to Start a Helping Session

Clients often have preconceived notions of what counseling is like. Television and movies contribute to popular images of bearded men smoking pipes and looking at clients lying on padded couches. Counselors are as different as are clients: they come in all shapes and sizes, and in both sexes. Counseling settings also vary from plush offices to storefronts. Although both counselors and counseling settings may differ considerably, effective helpers often follow similar approaches to beginning counseling sessions. At the start of a helping session, it is particularly important to try to reduce the client's concerns about the counseling situation. Good helpers make their clients feel as comfortable as possible from the very beginning of a counseling session.

It is best to have a helping session in a private room with a desk and at least two chairs. Other useful things to have in the room are paper, carbon paper, a clipboard, a pen, ashtrays, a clock or watch, a box of tissues, and a wastebasket.

Two activities should be done before a helping session: arrange the office furniture, and prepare a sheet of paper for ranking the alternatives identified.

Arrange Office Furniture

Arrange a desk and chair for yourself and a client in one of the ways shown in Figure 6. Other aspects of a comfortable counseling room include comfortable furniture and wall and room decorations. There should be no distractions. You should not have to answer the phone, and no one should enter the room once the door has been closed.

Note that the helper should not be directly behind the desk with the client on the other side of the desk, as this separates the parties unnecessarily. Nor should the helper sit on the desk or in a chair at a higher level than the client. Sitting at the same level promotes communication, which is the heart of an effective helping relationship.

Prepare a Problem-Solving Worksheet

To prepare the worksheet, follow the instructions in Chapter 10. Give yourself at least ten blank lines under the heading "Alternatives."

We recommend five activities in starting a helping session: invite the client into the office, ask the client to sit down, sit facing the client, exchange initial greetings, and explain confidentiality (this last is necessary only for the first session with the client).

Invite the Client into the Office

You should address the client by name, tell the client your name, look directly into the client's eyes, and smile. You may want to shake hands. Ask the client to come with you into your office, including "please" in your request. Walk toward your office. Make sure the client is following you. After you and the client have entered the office, close the door.

An example of how you can invite a client into the office is as follows:

• "Hello, Mr. Jones. My name is Sharon Leight." (*The helper is smiling at Mr. Jones and maintaining eye contact with him. She extends her hand to Mr. Jones and shakes his hand.*) "Please come with me." (*She walks to the office, enters the office with Mr. Jones, and closes the door.*)

The initial greeting is designed to make the client feel welcomed and to begin the session in a friendly manner.

Ask the Client to Sit Down

You should ask the client to sit down. Gesture with your hand or head toward the chair in which you would like the client to sit. We recommend smiling and including the word "please" in your request. Maintain eye contact with the client.

Examples of how to ask a client to sit down are as follows:

• "Please have a seat here." (*Point toward a chair*)

• "Sit here, please." (*Extend your hand toward a chair*)

Asking the client to sit down is another way to help the client feel welcomed and comfortable in the helping setting.

Sit Facing the Client

You should maintain eye contact, lean forward slightly in your chair, smile, and pause for about five seconds. This allows time for the client to ask questions or otherwise adjust to the helping setting.

Exchange Initial Greetings

You should offer and respond to initial greeting statements. Maintain eye contact and smile.

Examples of initial greetings are as follows:

• HELPER: How are you today?

• HELPER: That's a lovely dress.
  CLIENT: Thank you. I bought it in New York.
  HELPER: How long ago were you in New York?
  CLIENT: My husband and I took a vacation there last spring.

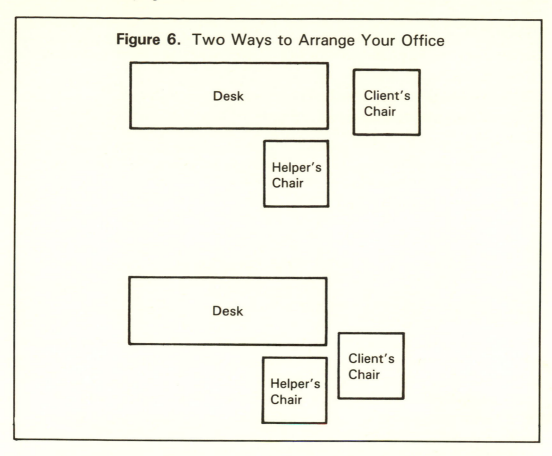

Figure 6. Two Ways to Arrange Your Office

An initial greeting demonstrates a friendliness that may be essential to the establishment of a helping relationship. It also helps break the ice during a time when the client is generally nervous.

Explain Confidentiality

You should state that anything discussed in the helping session will remain private information between you and the client. This is done only the first time you meet the client, unless he or she asks about confidentiality at another time.

Examples of how to explain confidentiality are:

- "Before we start, I want to make sure you understand that everything we talk about here is completely private and that no one else will know what we are discussing."

- "What we talk about will be just between you and me. You can feel sure that our sessions will remain confidential."

(Summary and Study Guide begin on page 82.)

SUMMARY

In summary, the steps in starting a helping session are as follows:

1. Arrange office furniture.
2. Prepare a sheet of paper for ranking alternatives identified.
3. Invite the client into the office.
4. Ask the client to sit down.
5. Sit facing the client.
6. Exchange initial greetings.
7. Explain confidentiality (first session only).

STUDY GUIDE

REVIEW QUESTIONS

Make sure you can answer all of the following questions. If you are unable to answer any question, reread that section of the chapter, and try the question again. It will be important that you know this information before beginning the practice sessions.

1. What materials are needed to begin a helping session?
2. A helper is recommended to do two activities before beginning a helping session.
   • What are these activities?
   • What does each activity involve?
3. Five activities that involve direct contact with the client are recommended in beginning a helping session.
   • What are these five activities?
   • What does each activity involve?

SKILLS PRACTICE

You and a partner may want to practice starting a helping session. This may be done by having the partner sit in a chair in a "waiting room" and having the student begin the role play by walking to the partner. Here is an example of how the partner might role play starting a helping session:

> **EXAMPLE**
> HELPER (Student): *Should arrange office furniture and prepare a Problem-Solving Worksheet.*
> CLIENT (Partner): (*Sits in a chair waiting for a counselor*)
> HELPER: *Should invite the client into the office.*
> CLIENT: (*Walks with the counselor*) Okay.
> HELPER: *Should ask the client to sit down.*
> CLIENT: (*Sits down in chair*) Thank you.

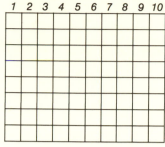

SKILLS CHECKLIST

Skill	Practice Session Number
	1 2 3 4 5 6 7 8 9 10
Arrange office furniture	
Prepare Problem-Solving Worksheet	
Invite client into office	
Ask client to sit down	
Sit facing client	
Exchange initial greetings	
Explain confidentiality	
Active listening	

✔ = well done; o = needs work

HELPER: *Should sit facing the client.*
CLIENT: (*Looks at helper and remains silent*)
HELPER: *Should exchange initial greetings.*
CLIENT: Fine. How are you?
HELPER: *Should explain confidentiality.*

Here are several exercises in which a student and a partner can practice the skill of starting a helping session.

► **EXERCISE 1**
You are an unmarried 22-year-old woman and have just learned that you are pregnant. You have come for help in deciding about having an abortion.

► **EXERCISE 2**
You want to break your lease with your landlord because he has failed to do needed repairs in your apartment. You would like the counselor to help you find out how to go about doing this.

► **EXERCISE 3**
You feel that you worry too much. You know it interferes with your ability to have fun, but don't know how to stop worrying. Your friends suggested you talk to someone about this problem, so you have come for help.

► **EXERCISE 4**
You have not been receiving your alimony payments, and have come for help in getting your ex-spouse to pay you regularly.

12

How to End a Helping Session

Earlier chapters addressed a variety of basic helping skills as well as considerations for opening helping sessions. This chapter focuses on aspects of closing these sessions. The end of a session often involves a review of what occurred during the session, suggestions for what the client should do between sessions, and completion of any other unfinished business. Closing a helping session successfully makes it much more likely that the client will return for further help when it is needed.

When to Use

End the helping session in the following situations:

- The problem-solving process has been completed.
- The end of an imposed time limit on a session is reached.
- The helper has all the information needed to work on the problem independently of the client.

There are seven activities in ending a helping session:

1. Make a summarizing statement.
2. Request feedback.
3. Request and answer client questions.
4. Schedule the next appointment.
5. Offer future help.
6. Make a final greeting.
7. Escort the client to the door.

1. Make a Summarizing Statement

You should use an appropriate summarizing initial phrase, describe the content of the discussion and any decision made, use an appropriate facial expression and posture. Then, you should pause.

An example of summarizing the session is:

- "Well, Charlie, we've talked about a lot of things today. You've decided you're going to go home and try to talk to your wife about these things and see if you can't both reach a mutually agreeable solution. Right?"

The summary provides a review of the helping session. It ties the main points together. Try to avoid discussing the feelings expressed in the session as you may not have adequate time to explore these feelings in the final minutes of a session.

2. Request Feedback

Ask the client to notify you about the outcome of the discussed problem. You may want to set a tentative date to talk to each other again.

Requesting feedback gives the helper information about the client's well-being after the helping session. It is another way you can make it easier for a client to return for further assistance, should that be necessary.

Examples of requesting feedback are as follows:

- "Please let me know how things work out."

- "I'd like to know how (*the chosen alternative*) works out. Could you come in after you try it and let me know?"

3. Request and Answer Client Questions

Ask the client a closed-ended question to determine if he or she has anything else to discuss. Try to answer those questions in a brief and honest manner.

Here are examples of requesting client questions:

- "Do you have any questions?"

- "Is there anything else you'd like to say?"

Asking for questions shows concern for the client's interests and demonstrates your willingness to take the time to be helpful.

After answering the client's question, you might ask again if there are any further questions. It's most helpful when you give your clients a chance to ask all the things they may have on their minds before ending the session.

4. Schedule the Next Appointment

If the helping session has resulted in the client's asking to come back or if there has been insufficient time to complete the problem-solving process, there may be a need for further help. When there is such a need, schedule the next appointment. You and the client should agree on a specific date and time to meet. Write this date and time on two pieces of paper—one for the client and one for yourself.

You might schedule the next appointment by saying:

- "When do you want to come in again?" or

- "How does (*date and time*) sound?"

5. Offer Future Help

You should state a willingness to provide further assistance to the client. Examples of offering future help include:

- "Don't hesitate to come back if there's anything else I can do."

- "Let me know if I can help you in the future."

Offering future help leaves the door open for later helping sessions. This may make it easier for the client to request help should it be needed at a later time.

6. Make a Final Greeting

You should make a final greeting statement while maintaining eye contact with the client and smiling. Here are some final greeting statements:

- "Good-bye."

- "It has been nice talking with you."

- "Let's keep in touch."

A final greeting demonstrates friendliness, which is essential in an effective helping relationship.

7. Escort the Client to the Door

You should open the door for the client and allow the client to walk through. This final courteous gesture further demonstrates respect and concern for the client.

If the helping session has completed the problem-solving process or the client is not interested in further help, more counseling may not be needed. When there is no need for further help, end the session by offering future help, making a final greeting, and escorting the client to the door.

Whether or not the client is to return, you should file your copy of the list of alternatives identified for solving his or her problem. Most counseling centers have some filing system to keep track of clients who have been seen for counseling. These files are often kept locked to insure confidentiality. Keeping a copy of the alternatives identified will provide you with a quick reminder should you meet with this client again later. It will help you make an accurate summarizing statement of this helping session the next time you see this client.

SUMMARY

In summary, the steps in ending a helping session are as follows:

1. Make a summarizing statement.

2. Request feedback.

3. Request and answer client questions.

4. If necessary, schedule the next appointment.

5. Offer future help.

6. Make a final greeting.

7. Escort the client to the door.

STUDY GUIDE

REVIEW QUESTIONS

Make sure you can answer all of the following questions. If you are unable to answer any question, reread that section of the chapter, and try the question again. It will be important that you know this information before beginning the practice session.

1. When should a helping session be ended?

2. If the helping session has resulted in the need for further help, the counselor should schedule another session. What does this involve?

3. There are six other activities in ending a helping session, in addition to scheduling another session.

   • What are these six activities?

   • What does each activity involve?

4. We have recommended that you do one last task at the end of a helping session, after the client has left your office.

   • What is this?

   • What does it involve?

SKILLS PRACTICE

You and a partner may want to practice ending a helping session. This may be done by using a list of alternative solutions identified during the problem-solving practice sessions. Here is an example of how the partner might role play ending a helping session:

EXAMPLE

HELPER (Student): *Should make a summarizing statement.*
CLIENT (Partner): That's right.
HELPER: *Should request feedback.*
CLIENT: I certainly will. I sure hope it helps.
HELPER: *Should request client questions.*
CLIENT: I'm wondering . . . can anyone come here for help?
HELPER: *Should answer client's question and ask if client has any other questions.*

(Example continues on page 88.)

SKILLS CHECKLIST

Skill

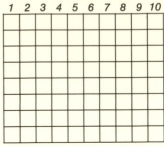

	Practice Session Number
	1 2 3 4 5 6 7 8 9 10

Make summarizing statement
Request feedback
Request client questions
Answer client questions
Schedule next appointment (if needed)
Offer future help
Make final greeting
Escort client to door

↙ = well done; o = needs work

CLIENT: None that I can think of now.
HELPER: *Should offer future help.*
CLIENT: Thank you. I really appreciate your interest.
HELPER: *Should make a final greeting.*
CLIENT: Good-bye.
HELPER: *Should escort the client to the door.*

Here are several exercises in which a student and a partner can practice the skill of ending a helping session:

EXERCISE 1
You've had a lengthy discussion about the problems you've had in finding proper care for your elderly mother. You've decided to take her into your home until she can move into a satisfactory nursing home.

EXERCISE 2
You have been very depressed and, during the counseling session, were unable to identify the source of your problem or find anything that sounded useful to do.

EXERCISE 3
You are new to the community, and came to find out more about it. You've been given a great deal of information about the recreational activities in the area.

EXERCISE 4
After a long session talking about your dissatisfaction with your marriage, you decide you would like to return to the counselor and to bring your wife with you.

13

Putting It All Together

This chapter includes a written exercise and practice opportunities designed to help you put together all of the helping skills you have learned. For the written exercise, read the situation below, and complete the blanks with an *example* of what you would say or do if you were actually responding to a client in a helping situation. For example, you might respond to the requirement "Arrange the office" with the answer, "I would move the chairs so that we could face each other." "Exchange initial greeting" might be answered: "Hello, Mr. Williams, I am Jane Marconi. It's good to see you."

Mrs. Susan Black, who lives near the Highland Multipurpose Center, has dropped in to talk with someone about a problem. She appears to be about 45 years of age and of good health, although she looks rather tired. You receive a call in your upstairs office that Mrs. Black is on her way to see you.

1. **Arrange the office:**

   a. _____

   _____

   b. _____

   _____

   MRS. BLACK: (*Arrives at the door of your office.*)

2. **Invite the client into the office:** _____

   _____

   MRS. BLACK: (*Steps inside the office.*)

3. **Ask client to sit down:** _____

   MRS. BLACK: (*Sits down in a chair across from you.*)

4. **Sit facing client:** _____

5. **Exchange initial greetings:** _____

   MRS. BLACK: I'm Susan Black. Pleased to meet you.

6. **Explain confidentiality:** _____

_____

7. **Request problem statement with open-ended question:** _____

_____

MRS. BLACK: My husband is always yelling at me. When I tell him to stop, he
sometimes hits me. I just don't know what to do.

8. **Define problem:** _____

_____

MRS. BLACK: Yeah, that's about it.

9. **Explain problem-solving process:** _____

_____

10. **State usefulness of the process:** _____

_____

11. **Ask client for alternative solutions:** _____

_____

MRS. BLACK: Well, I suppose I could leave him.

12. **Identify other alternatives:** _____

_____

MRS. BLACK: I have thought about asking him to see a counselor.

13. **Identify other alternatives:** _____

MRS. BLACK: I wonder if we couldn't take that vacation away from the kids that
we have been talking about. That's all the ideas that I can think of.

14. **Add other alternatives:** _____

_____

MRS. BLACK: Talking this over with his parents is a good idea.

15. **Summarize alternatives identified and turn the list to the client:** _____

_____

_____

_____

_____

MRS. BLACK: Those things are worth thinking about.

16. **Analyze consequences of first alternative:** _____

_____

MRS. BLACK: Leaving him would hurt too much. I still love him.

17. **Analyze consequences of second alternative:** _____

_____

MRS. BLACK: I suppose that a counselor could help, though it would be expensive.

18. **Analyze consequences of third alternative:** _____

_____

MRS. BLACK: The vacation would be fun, though neither of us could get away from work now.

19. **Analyze consequences of final alternative:** _____

_____

MRS. BLACK: His parents would talk to him, but he would be mad at me for telling them. Well, that pretty well covers the good and bad things that would happen if I follow these ideas.

20. **Rate the first alternative:** _____
MRS. BLACK: No, I can't do that.

21. **Rate the second alternative:** _____
MRS. BLACK: That's a good idea.

22. **Rate the third alternative:** _____
MRS. BLACK: The vacation is not possible right now.

23. **Rate the final alternative:** _____
MRS. BLACK: Sneaking behind his back isn't a good idea.

24. **Select the best alternative:** _____
MRS. BLACK: It seems to me that getting counseling for both of us is the best idea. But, you know, I can't tell you how much it hurts to talk about these things.

25. **Reflecting statement:** _____

_____

MRS. BLACK: His father was just like him. He beat his wife.

26. **Listen actively:** _____
MRS. BLACK: I just wish I knew that this would work. (*Begins to cry.*)

27. **Reflecting statement:** _____

_____

MRS. BLACK: It's terrible not knowing whether your husband will be screaming when you get home. It's very upsetting to the children. (*Pauses for a long time.*)

28. **Reflecting statement:** _____

_____

MRS. BLACK: I'm doing all right now. I think that talking with you has helped. (*Smiles slightly.*)

29. **Determine client satisfaction with the choice:** _____

_____

MRS. BLACK: Yes, I am satisfied that the counseling idea may help.

30. **State support for client decision:** _____

_____

31. **Ask if help is needed to take action:** _____

_____

MRS. BLACK: Thank you, but I think that I will be able to handle it myself.

32. **Summarize the session:** _____

_____

_____

_____

MRS. BLACK: That's a pretty good description of what we talked about.

33. **Request client questions:** _____

_____

MRS. BLACK: One question. Are there people at the County Mental Health Center that I could call about this?

34. **Answer client questions:** _____

_____

35. **Request feedback:** _____

_____

MRS. BLACK: Yes, I will be sure to let you know.

36. **Offer future help:** _____
MRS. BLACK: Thank you.

37. **Make final greeting:** _____

    MRS. BLACK: Goodbye, and thanks again.

38. **Escort client to the door.**

39. **Place list of alternatives in the file.**

STUDY GUIDE

SKILLS PRACTICE

Here are an example and several exercises in which a student and a partner can practice all of the counseling skills. For additional practice, you can create your own situations. Here is an example of how a partner might role play a problem situation to provide practice for the entire set of skills:

EXAMPLE

HELPER (Student): *should arrange office furniture and prepare sheet for ranking alternatives:*

- *Invite client into office.*
- *Ask the client to sit down.*
- *Sit facing client.*
- *Exchange initial greetings.*
- *Explain confidentiality.*

CLIENT (Partner): (*Looking very worried*) I haven't had a steady job in six months. I feel really insecure about money. It's getting on my nerves.

HELPER: *Should make verbal encouragement or reflecting statement.*

CLIENT: My family is dependent upon my salary, and I feel terrible that it's been so long since I've contributed anything to the household.

HELPER: *Should make verbal encouragement or ask question.*

CLIENT: (*Continues the conversation*)

HELPER: *Should do problem-solving activities:*

- *Request problem statement.*
- *Define problem.*
- *Explain problem-solving process.*
- *State usefulness of process.*
- *Identify alternative solutions.*
- *Summarize alternatives identified.*
- *Turn list to client.*

(Study Guide continues on page 94.)

- *Analyze consequences of each alternative.*
- *Select best alternative.*
- *Determine client's satisfaction with choice.*
- *State support for decision.*
- *Ask if help is needed to take action.*
- *If it is needed, provide help in taking action.*

HELPER: *Should do closing activities:*

- *Summarize session.*
- *Request and answer client questions.*
- *Request feedback.*
- *Offer future help.*
- *Make final greeting.*
- *Escort client to door.*
- *Place list of alternatives in file.*

► EXERCISE 1

You are a senior citizen (aged 67) and are worried about your financial security in your old age. You receive a small pension, but want help in planning your financial future.

► EXERCISE 2

You are very dissatisfied with the way you look. You have come to the counselor to talk about this and get some ideas of how you can get yourself motivated to do things to help you look better.

► EXERCISE 3

You have just decided to go back to work, but still have a young child at home. You have come to the center in hopes of finding information about day care or other facilities available where you can leave you child while you are at work. Even though you are excited about going back to work, you feel a bit guilty about not being home with your child.

► EXERCISE 4

You are a student coming for counseling because you get nervous before taking tests, and you know this is lowering your grades. You've tried everything you can think of to stop yourself from getting so nervous, but nothing has worked. You are hoping counseling will help.

SKILLS CHECKLIST

Skill

Practice Session Number

1 2 3 4 5 6 7 8 9 10

Opening
Arrange office furniture
Prepare Problem-Solving Worksheet
Invite client into office
Ask client to sit down
Sit facing client
Exchange initial greetings
Explain confidentiality

Problem Solving
Request problem statement
Define problem
Explain problem-solving process
State usefulness of process
Identify alternative solutions
    Ask client first
    Introduce yours in open-ended manner
Summarize alternatives
Turn list to client
Analyze consequences of each alternative
Rate each alternative
Select best alternative
Determine client satisfaction with choice
Identify other alternatives if not satisfied
State support of decision
Ask if help is needed to take action
Provide help (if needed)

General
Listen actively
Make reflecting statements and pauses
Make open-ended questions and pauses
Make closed-ended questions and pauses
Make summarizing statements

Closing
Summarize session
Request feedback
Request client questions
Answer client questions
Schedule next appointment (if needed)
Offer future help
Make final greeting
Escort client to door
File Problem-Solving Worksheet

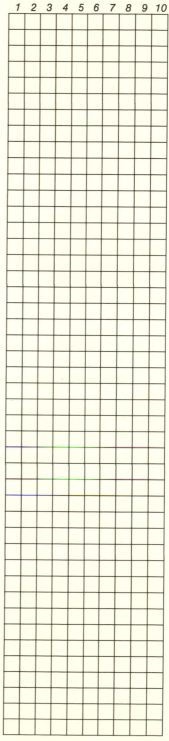

✔ = well done; o = needs work

14

Epilogue

So, now you are on your way toward being a skilled helper. You have learned some effective ways of counseling clients and helping them analyze their problems. These skills will help you to establish a trusting relationship with the client. Within this counselor-client relationship, you will be able to assist the client in understanding the problem, identifying various ways to improve the situation, and making a decision about what to do.

Our students are usually quite excited with the prospect of using what they have learned to help others solve their problems. We share your excitement! However, such enthusiasm can lead to misuse of these skills. To use your newly learned skills responsibly, we encourage you to consider the issues in this chapter.

THINGS TO CONSIDER

1. It is your responsibility to keep confidential the information shared by a client. Helpers should never discuss the names of people or their problems unless permission is given by the client.

2. Students often gain a considerable degree of confidence following training in counseling and problem-solving skills. This increased confidence is desirable and expected. However, it is important that students understand that this limited training program does not qualify them as professionally trained counselors. Professionally trained counselors are required to have completed many years of training and supervision in counseling and are educated in theories of human development, personality, and pathology. This helps them deal effectively with a variety of psychological disorders and situational problems.

   There may be counseling situations in which the advanced skills and experience of a professionally trained counselor, psychologist, or psychiatrist are required. Good medical doctors do not hesitate to seek the advice or help of a specialist. We encourage you to seek out professional advice or help for any situation you feel unable to handle. Making a referral to a professional helper can be a wise helping decision.

   When should you make such a referral? Professional counseling should be recommended whenever a client is severely depressed, agitated, and/or nervous; makes any mention of killing or harming himself, herself, or someone else; abuses alcohol or other drugs; makes incoherent, nonsensical statements; mentions seeing visions or hearing imaginary voices; demonstrates bizarre behavior; has a severe marital or family problem; requests medication; or requests psychiatric or psychotherapeutic help. Moreover, refer a client to a professional anytime you feel afraid or unable to handle the client's problem. You should know that there are times when *all* counselors, even well-trained and experienced ones, feel unable to handle a counseling situation on their own. A good counselor knows his or her abilities, and does not feel embarrassed or afraid to ask for help or to refer a client to a more experienced helper. It's better to be safe than sorry! Here are some statements you can make in such a situation:

- "I think it might be helpful for you to talk with a professional. I'm going to refer you to _____."

- "I'm worried about you, and I think it would help you to talk to a professional. May I help you set up an appointment?"

- "I'm sorry, but I seem to be unable to help you. I'm going to refer you to a professionally trained person who, I think, will be better able to help you."

3. Helpers may be inclined to offer advice to clients rather than help the clients explore options for solving the problem. People frequently come for counseling assistance because they are bombarded with advice and need help sorting through all the opinions. Students may be inclined to offer their own suggestions to clients. Resist offering advice! The consequences of a client's actions rest largely with him or her (and not with the helper). Giving advice or telling a client what to do is usually perceived by a client as *un*helpful. Clients have a tendency not to follow many helper-offered suggestions anyway.

4. Students frequently wonder where and when they should use their new counseling skills. Many of the skills are really just good communication skills, and can be used in many situations. The helping skills described in this text are applicable in a variety of encounters with family, friends, and neighbors. Professional and nonprofessional helpers are employed in many settings, including hospitals, schools, and community centers. So you should be able to use these helping skills with friends, family, or in work-related helping situations.

5. The consumer is always right. If your friends or relatives do not like the way you interact with them in helping situations, then you are not helping properly. They may prefer your previous style of interaction to your attempts to use these helping skills. Alternatively, their complaints may indicate that you are trying to be a helper in situations in which your help was not requested. You should consider limiting your use of the helping skills with these particular persons or situations. With more practice, the helping skills will become more natural. As they become natural, you may find that friends and relatives enjoy speaking with you even more because you have become such a good listener and a helpful resource.

6. You may find yourself being helped by learning these helping skills. For example, you may find that people respond to you in a more open and positive way when you use these counseling skills. This seems to be one of the benefits of more effective helping.

7. You should consider that any choice a client makes will probably have some impact on other persons. For example, should a mother who is dissatisfied with her child's teacher decide to talk to the school principal, there is the chance that the teacher might resent this and take it out on the child. Though such a possible consequence

might have been discussed with the client, the resulting impact of a client action on others may still come as a surprise. Accordingly, it may be helpful to encourage clients to analyze fully what effect on others, as well as themselves, each identified alternative may have.

8. Though immediately after training you may recall these helping skills easily, you may forget some in time. To continue to be a skilled helper, it is important that you practice your newly learned skills, referring to this text as necessary for follow-up training. If your helping skills are used only infrequently, you might retain your helping effectiveness by role playing helping situations periodically. Refer to the practice checklist at the end of Chapter 13 to remind you of some of the essential counseling and problem-solving skills used in helping situations. Some of our students put a copy of this checklist on their desks to help remember the helping skills.

9. No training program can include all of the skills, information, and wisdom required to help with the array of troubles your friends and clients may discuss with you. In bringing your own unique strengths to helping, you extend the guidance offered in this book. As you gain experience with these skills, you will further the practice of helping beyond what we have been able to describe.

   Finally, you are on your own. Congratulations on your success in learning these helping skills! Welcome to the growing community of skilled helpers! To paraphrase the words of the poet Edgar Guest,

> *May God grant you the serenity to accept the things with which you cannot help, courage to help with the things you can, and wisdom to know the difference.*

PART III

PROBLEM-
SOLVING
INDEX

15

Introduction to the Index

DESCRIPTION OF THE INDEX

The Problem-Solving Index is provided to assist you in helping a client solve a problem. The Index is divided into two sections. Section I, "Everyday Problems and Alternative Solutions to Them," lists more than 250 specific problems for which people request help. Each problem is alphabetically categorized under the headings of Education, Family and Friends, Financial, Health, Housing, Occupation, and Self-Improvement. Each specific problem is followed by a list of possible alternative solutions. This should help you in assisting a client in identifying alternatives to solve his or her problem.

Section II of the Index, "The Alternative Solutions and Their Possible Consequences," lists possible consequences, both positive and negative, that might occur were the client to select the alternative solution. This should help you in assisting a client to analyze the consequences of each alternative, and should, in turn, help the client make the best decision.

The Index is not inclusive. There may be problems people discuss with you that are not listed. You may be able to think of effective alternative solutions. It seems best to use the Index as a resource, a tool in helping a client solve a problem.

HOW TO USE THE INDEX

At the beginning of Section I is a master list of all the everyday problems included in Section I. Scanning this may help you quickly locate the specific problem being discussed. Section II similarly begins with a master list of all the alternative solutions and their possible consequences included in Section II.

In the main part of Section I, each alternative solution to a problem is followed by a number. This number refers you to the appropriate item in Section II, which lists both the positive and negative consequences that might occur if a client were to select that particular alternative.

16

Section I: Everyday Problems and Alternative Solutions to Them

MASTER LIST OF ITEMS IN SECTION I

Following is a list of the everyday problems dealt with in this section in the order in which they appear.

Education

1. Advanced education--deciding about it
2. Child care--needs child care while at school
3. Day care--needs information about day care
4. Discipline--child is discipline problem in school
5. Dislikes school--but wants to graduate
6. Dislikes school--thinking of quitting
7. Expelled from school
8. Graduate Equivalency Diploma-- wants to complete
9. G. I. Benefits--questions about education benefits
10. Grades--child has poor grades
11. Grades--have gotten worse
12. Graduate school--unsure about whether to attend
13. Graduated--unsure what to do next
14. Learning difficulties--child has learning difficulties in school
15. Military--wants information about military
16. Military--questions about G. I. Benefits
17. Nursery schools--needs information about nursery schools
18. Peer problem--child having peer difficulties in school
19. Pregnant student--problems in school
20. Studying--child has poor study habits
21. Studying--child doesn't like to study
22. Studying--no place to study at home
23. Subjects--not interested in some subjects
24. Teacher problem--parents having problem with child's teacher
25. Test taking--anxious about, is affecting grades
26. Trade school--wants to learn a trade
27. Training--lacks training for a job
28. Truancy--child skips school
29. Vocational training school--wants to go

Family and Friends

30. Abortion
31. Alcohol--child abuses alcohol
32. Alcohol--parent abuses alcohol

33. Alcohol--spouse abuses alcohol
34. Child--emotional problems caused by divorce
35. Child--emotional problems due to parents' separation
36. Child--not getting along with brother or sister
37. Child--not getting along with parents
38. Child--peer problems in school
39. Child unhappy--parents want help
40. Child violent--parents want help
41. Child abuse--by neighbor
42. Child abuse--by spouse
43. Child care--needs child care services
44. Child support problems
45. Death--of parent or spouse causing emotional problems
46. Death--of parent or spouse causing financial problems
47. Discipline--problem disciplining child
48. Divorce--emotional problems in one spouse
49. Divorce--causing financial problems
50. Divorce--wants help deciding about getting divorced
51. Drugs--child abuses drugs
52. Drugs--parent abuses drugs
53. Drugs--spouse abuses drugs
54. Illegitimate child--causing emotional problems in mother or child
55. Illegitimate child--causing financial problems
56. Injury--to family member causing emotional problems to injured member
57. Injury--to family member causing family financial problems
58. Injury--to family member causing emotional problems to non-injured members
59. In-laws--interfering
60. Job--family member unable to find work
61. Leave home--for child who wants to leave home
62. Marital problems--unhappy in marriage
63. Marriage--wants help deciding about getting married
64. Marriage falling apart
65. Parent--aging parent needs care

66. Parents--child feels he or she cannot talk about certain problems with parents
67. Parents--child feels parents are too strict or old-fashioned
68. Parents--child feels parents don't understand him or her
69. Parents--fight too much
70. Parents--interfering
71. Pregnant daughter--school problems
72. Retarded child--problems raising retarded child
73. Runaway--child has run away
74. Runaway--child threatens to run away
75. Senile adult
76. Separation--causing financial problems
77. Separation--emotional problems in one spouse
78. Separation--wants help deciding about getting separated
79. Spouse--doesn't help enough with home
80. Spouse--feels spouse is not home enough
81. Spouses--fighting over child rearing
82. Spouses--fighting over money
83. Spouse--not helping enough with child rearing
84. Spouse violent--spouse wants help
85. Working too hard--worried because family member is working too hard

Financial

86. Alimony--not receiving payments
87. Bankruptcy
88. Budgeting--needs help budgeting better
89. Cash--needs money
90. Child support payments--not receiving
91. Clothing--needs money for
92. Death--of parent or spouse causing financial problems
93. Disabled veteran--needs money
94. Divorce--causing financial problems
95. Electricity--needs money for
96. Education--needs money to continue education

97. Financially dependent—doesn't like it
98. Food—needs money for
99. Furniture—needs money for
100. Gas—needs money for
101. Home improvements—needs money for
102. Housing—needs money for
103. Illegitimate child—causing financial problems
104. Income—no steady income
105. Injury to family member causing family financial problems
106. Insurance—needs money for
107. Jail—needs money to get someone out of jail
108. Legal advice—needs money for
109. Loan—needs information about how to get one
110. Loan—needs loan to buy home
111. Loan consolidation—needs to arrange
112. Medical supplies—needs money for
113. Money—needs money
114. Money—has less money than friends
115. Money—spending too much money
116. Old age—worried about financial security in old age
117. Rent—needs money for
118. Separation—causing financial problems
119. Social security insurance problems
120. Tax problems
121. Telephone—needs money for
122. Transportation—needs money for
123. Unemployment compensation—late or denied
124. Veteran—wants to get veteran's benefits
125. Water—needs money for
126. Welfare—deciding whether or not to get a job
127. Welfare—delays in receiving checks
128. Welfare—wants adjustment in welfare allowance
129. Welfare—whether or not to apply for
130. Workmen's Compensation—late or denied

Health

131. Abortion—needs information
132. Aches
133. Alcohol—related problems
134. Allergy problems
135. Anxiety problems
136. Appetite problems
137. Birth control—needs information
138. Depression
139. Dizziness
140. Drug-related problems
141. Eye trouble
142. Headaches
143. Heart trouble
144. High blood pressure
145. Injury—causing emotional problems
146. Insane—thoughts of going insane
147. Medicaid—not receiving service
148. Medical supplies—needs money for
149. Medicare—not receiving service
150. Memory is poor
151. Menstruation problems
152. Nervousness
153. Overweight
154. Physical pains
155. Pregnancy—needs medical care
156. Pregnancy—needs pregnancy test
157. Rape—causing emotional problems
158. Rape—causing physical problems
159. Sexual problems
160. Sleeping problems
161. Stomach problems
162. Suicidal thoughts or attempts
163. Tired too much of the time
164. Tobacco—related problems
165. Underweight
166. Venereal disease
167. Worry—worry becoming a health problem

Housing

168. Electricity—needs money for
169. Eviction notice
170. Furniture—needs money for
171. Gas off—needs money for
172. Home improvement—needs help to do

173. Home improvement--needs money for
174. Housing--needs a place to live
175. Housing--needs place to stay temporarily
176. Housing--poor housing conditions
177. Housing--wants to buy home
178. Housing--wants to rent
179. Landlord--raised rent
180. Landlord--tenant wants to break lease
181. Landlord--wants to sell house
182. Landlord--won't make repairs
183. Living with relatives--causing problems
184. Loan--needs loan to buy home
185. Money--needs money for housing
186. Privacy--lacking privacy in living situation
187. Rent--needs money for
188. Telephone--needs money for
189. Undesirable location--living in undesirable location
190. Water--needs money for

Occupation

191. Child care--needed while working
192. Combining housework, children and job
193. Graduated--unsure what to do next
194. Job--no advancement at present job
195. Job--discrimination problem on job
196. Job--dissatisfied with present job
197. Job--does not know how to find a job
198. Job--doesn't know what kind to do
199. Job--fired from job
200. Job--needs information about job openings
201. Job--wants information about specific job
202. Job--lacks training or experience
203. Job--may lose job
204. Job--needs a job
205. Job--has poor work history, but needs job
206. Job--transportation problem to work
207. Military--wants information about military
208. Own business--wants own business
209. Part-time job--wants one
210. Refuses to work--family member refusing
211. Shift changed--caused problems at home
212. Supervisor--problems at work
213. Trade--wants to learn a trade

Self-Improvement

214. Alone too much
215. Anger problem--hard to handle anger
216. Appearance--wants to improve appearance
217. Conversations--trouble talking to people
218. Decisions--has difficulty making decisions
219. Depressed
220. Disappointed in self
221. Disliking someone
222. Disliked by someone
223. Failing--afraid of
224. Friends--unable to make friends
225. Graduate Equivalency Diploma-- wants to obtain
226. Habit--wants to break a habit
227. Hobbies
228. Inferior--feels inferior to others
229. Jealous
230. Lazy--not getting anything done
231. Legal advice--wants to obtain
232. Lonely
233. Made fun of--being made fun of by others
234. Marital counseling--wants to obtain
235. Medical services--wants to obtain
236. Nervous with people of opposite sex
237. Nervous with people of same sex
238. Nervous--worrying too much
239. Overweight
240. Procrastinating
241. Professional counseling--wants to obtain
242. Recreation--doesn't do enough
243. Religious beliefs--confused by beliefs
244. Self-confidence--lacking
245. Shy--feels too shy
246. Social life--not enough
247. Speech trouble

248. Temper problems
249. Time--not using time satis-
     factorily
250. Tutor--wants to obtain
251. Underweight

252. Unhappy
253. Unpopular--feels unpopular;
     wants to be more popular
254. Violent--gets violent when
     mad

PROBLEMS AND THEIR SOLUTIONS

Education

1. ADVANCED EDUCATION--
   DECIDING ABOUT IT

Alternative solutions:

(1) Find a job, and see if you
    like the work 14
(2) Talk to guidance counselor . . 49
(3) Write for catalogues and
    information 50
(4) Go to public library for
    information 12
(5) Talk to family and friends
    for advice 51
(6) Talk to working people 15
(7) Be a part-time student 52

2. CHILD CARE--NEEDS CHILD CARE
   WHILE AT SCHOOL

See: "OCCUPATIONAL PROBLEMS"

     Child Care

3. DAY CARE--NEEDS INFORMATION
   ABOUT DAY CARE

Alternative solutions:

(1) Talk to family and friends
    for advice 51
(2) Look in Yellow Pages and
    newspaper 62
(3) Talk to the principal 48
(4) Call the local churches 63

4. DISCIPLINE--CHILD IS
   DISCIPLINE PROBLEM IN SCHOOL

Alternative solutions:

(1) Talk to the teacher 41
(2) Talk to school psychologist . . 42
(3) Talk to a professional
    counselor 13

(4) Ignore the problem, wait and
    hope 11
(5) Talk to family member about
    problem 47
(6) Help child establish new
    activities and hobbies 174
(7) Find a tutor 46
(8) Punish child 44

5. DISLIKES SCHOOL--BUT WANTS
   TO GRADUATE

Alternative solutions:

(1) Do the best that you can in
    school 55
(2) Quit school, and take Graduate
    Equivalency Diploma for a high
    school degree 56
(3) Quit school, and take time off . 53

6. DISLIKES SCHOOL--THINKING
   OF QUITTING

Alternative solutions:

(1) Quit school, and take time off . 53
(2) Quit school, and find a job . . 54
(3) Do the best that you can in
    school 55
(4) Quit school, and take Graduate
    Equivalency Diploma for a high
    school degree 56
(5) Talk to a guidance counselor . . 49
(6) Don't take subjects you don't
    like 57
(7) Find a tutor 46

7. EXPELLED FROM SCHOOL

Alternative solutions:

(1) Talk to the principal 48
(2) Quit school, and take time off . 53

(3) Transfer to a different school . 58
(4) Find a tutor 46
(5) Talk to a guidance counselor . . 49

8. GRADUATE EQUIVALENCY DIPLOMA--
WANTS TO COMPLETE

Alternative solutions:

(1) Talk to a guidance counselor . . 49
(2) Find a tutor 46
(3) Go to public library for
information 12

9. G. I. BENEFITS--QUESTIONS
ABOUT EDUCATION BENEFITS

See: "EDUCATION PROBLEMS"

Military--G. I. Benefits

10. GRADES--CHILD HAS POOR GRADES

See: "EDUCATION PROBLEMS"

Studying--Child has poor
study habits

11. GRADES--HAVE GOTTEN WORSE

Alternative solutions:

(1) Continue to let grades get
worse 59
(2) Ignore the problem, wait and
hope 11
(3) Talk to guidance counselor
to change program or about
grades 60
(4) Talk to the teacher 41
(5) Improve your study habits . . . 61
(6) Talk to a professional
counselor 13
(7) Go to public library for
information 12
(8) Improve your study habits . . . 61
(9) Find a tutor 46

12. GRADUATE SCHOOL--UNSURE ABOUT
WHETHER TO ATTEND

See: "EDUCATION PROBLEMS"

Advanced education

13. GRADUATED--UNSURE WHAT TO
DO NEXT

Alternative solutions:

(1) Find a new job 6
(2) Go to school 17

(3) Talk to a professional
counselor 13
(4) Talk to a guidance counselor . 49

14. LEARNING DIFFICULTIES--CHILD
HAS LEARNING DIFFICULTIES
IN SCHOOL

Alternative solutions:

(1) Talk to the teacher 41
(2) Talk to school psychologist . . 42
(3) Find a tutor 46

15. MILITARY--WANTS INFORMATION
ABOUT MILITARY

See: "OCCUPATION PROBLEMS"

Military

16. MILITARY--QUESTIONS ABOUT
G. I. BENEFITS

Alternative solutions:

(1) Call area Veterans Administration Office 68
(2) Call local recruiter 38
(3) Contact League of Women
Voters, Red Cross, Salvation
Army, Council of Churches . . .107

17. NURSERY SCHOOLS--NEEDS
INFORMATION ABOUT
NURSERY SCHOOLS

See: "EDUCATION PROBLEMS"

Day Care

18. PEER PROBLEM--CHILD HAVING
PEER DIFFICULTIES IN SCHOOL

Alternative solutions:

(1) Talk to the teacher 41
(2) Talk to school psychologist . . 42
(3) Talk to a professional
counselor 13
(4) Ignore the problem, wait and
hope 11
(5) Talk to family member about
problem 47
(6) Help child establish new
activities and hobbies 174

19. PREGNANT STUDENT--PROBLEMS
IN SCHOOL

Alternative solutions:

(1) Talk to a guidance counselor . 49

(2) Talk to a school nurse 74
(3) Talk to the principal 48
(4) Obtain legal assistance 9
(5) Drop out of school 75
(6) Ignore the problem, wait and
    hope 11

20. STUDYING--CHILD HAS POOR STUDY HABITS

Alternative solutions:

(1) Ignore the problem, wait and
    hope 11
(2) Talk to school psychologist . . 42
(3) Talk to the teacher 41
(4) Find a tutor 46
(5) Try to teach child better study
    habits 43
(6) Punish child 44
(7) Reward child for good behavior . 45
(8) Talk to a professional
    counselor 13

21. STUDYING--CHILD DOESN'T LIKE TO STUDY

See: "EDUCATION PROBLEMS"

      Studying--Child has poor
      study habits

22. STUDYING--NO PLACE TO STUDY AT HOME

Alternative solutions:

(1) Study in library or other
    place besides home 64
(2) Arrange with family for time
    and place to study at home . . . 65

23. SUBJECTS--NOT INTERESTED IN SOME SUBJECTS

Alternative solutions:

(1) Don't take subjects you don't
    like 57
(2) Talk to guidance counselor to
    change program or about grades . 60
(3) Don't attend classes 66
(4) Do the best that you can in
    school 55
(5) Find a tutor 46

24. TEACHER PROBLEM--PARENTS HAVING PROBLEM WITH CHILD'S TEACHER

Alternative solutions:

(1) Talk to the principal 48
(2) Talk to the teacher 41
(3) Ignore the problem, wait and
    hope 11
(4) Change teachers 67
(5) Threaten person involved . . .155

25. TEST TAKING--ANXIOUS ABOUT, IS AFFECTING GRADES

Alternative solutions:

(1) Talk to the teacher 41
(2) Talk to school psychologist . . 42
(3) Talk to a professional
    counselor 13
(4) Improve your study habits . . . 61
(5) Ignore the problem, wait and
    hope 11
(6) Find a tutor 46

26. TRADE SCHOOL--WANTS TO LEARN A TRADE

Alternative solutions:

(1) Look in Yellow Pages and
    newspaper 62
(2) Relocate to attend vocational
    school 87
(3) Ask for on-the-job training . . 16
(4) Try to teach yourself a trade . 69
(5) Talk to a guidance counselor . 49
(6) Go to public library for
    information 12
(7) Contact state employment,
    school placement, and Veteran
    Administration offices 23

27. TRAINING--LACKS TRAINING FOR A JOB

See: "OCCUPATION PROBLEMS"

      Training

28. TRUANCY--CHILD SKIPS SCHOOL

Alternative solutions:

(1) Talk to family member about
    problem 47
(2) Punish child 44

(3) Talk to the principal 48
(4) Talk to school psychologist . . 42
(5) Talk to a professional
    counselor 13
(6) Ignore the problem, wait and
    hope 11
(7) Threaten person involved . . .155

29. VOCATIONAL TRAINING SCHOOL-- WANTS TO GO

See: "EDUCATIONAL PROBLEMS"

    Trade School

Family and Friends

30. ABORTION

See: "HEALTH PROBLEMS"

    Abortion--Needs Information

31. ALCOHOL--CHILD ABUSES ALCOHOL

Alternative solutions:

(1) Talk to a professional
    counselor 13
(2) Talk to a physician 82
(3) Punish child 44
(4) Ignore the problem, wait and
    hope 11
(5) Talk to family member about
    the problem 47
(6) Talk to family and friends
    for advice 51
(7) Call the local churches 63
(8) Talk to a professional
    counselor 13
(9) Ask parent, spouse, or child
    to leave the home 83
(10) Call area chapters of Alanon .172
(11) Call local crisis hot-line . .173
(12) Threaten person involved . . .155

32. ALCOHOL--PARENT ABUSES ALCOHOL

Alternative solutions:

(1) Talk to a professional
    counselor 13
(2) Ask parent, spouse, or child
    to leave the home 83
(3) Talk to family and friends
    for advice 51
(4) Ignore the problem, wait and
    hope 11
(5) Call the local churches 63
(6) Tell your parents how the
    situation is affecting you . .127

(7) Talk to a physician 82
(8) Call area chapters of Alanon .172
(9) Call local crisis hot-line . .173
(10) Threaten person involved . . .155

33. ALCOHOL--SPOUSE ABUSES ALCOHOL

Alternative solutions:

(1) Talk to a professional
    counselor 13
(2) Talk to a physician 82
(3) Ignore the problem, wait and
    hope 11
(4) Ask parent, spouse, or child
    to leave the home 83
(5) Talk to family friends for
    advice 51
(6) Call the local churches 63
(7) Call area chapters of Alanon .172
(8) Call local crisis hot-line . .173
(9) Threaten person involved . . .155

34. CHILD--EMOTIONAL PROBLEMS CAUSED BY DIVORCE

Alternative solutions:

(1) Talk to a professional
    counselor 13
(2) Talk to a minister, priest,
    or rabbi for help 89
(3) Ignore the problem, wait and
    hope 11
(4) Help child establish new
    activities and hobbies 174

35. CHILD--EMOTIONAL PROBLEMS DUE TO PARENTS' SEPARATION

See: "FAMILY AND FRIENDS PROBLEMS"

    Child--Emotional problems
    caused by divorce

36. CHILD--NOT GETTING ALONG WITH
    BROTHER OR SISTER

Alternative solutions:

(1) Punish child 44
(2) Talk to family member about
    problem 47
(3) Talk to a professional
    counselor 13
(4) Talk to family and friends for
    advice 51
(5) Ask child to move out 156
(6) Help child establish new
    activities and hobbies 174
(7) Set aside time to be together .100

37. CHILD--NOT GETTING ALONG
    WITH PARENTS

Alternative solutions:

(1) Punish child 44
(2) Talk to family member about
    the problem 47
(3) Talk to family and friends
    for advice 51
(4) Talk to a professional
    counselor 13
(5) Ask child to move out 156
(6) Ignore the problem, wait and
    hope 11
(7) Set aside time to be together .100
(8) Complain 166

38. CHILD--PEER PROBLEMS IN SCHOOL

See: "EDUCATION PROBLEMS"

      Peer Problem--Child having
      peer difficulties in school

39. CHILD UNHAPPY--PARENTS
    WANT HELP

Alternative solutions:

(1) Talk to the teacher 41
(2) Talk to minister, priest, or
    rabbi for help 89
(3) Talk to a professional
    counselor 13
(4) Talk to school psychologist . . 42
(5) Talk to family and friends
    for advice 51
(6) Ignore the problem, wait and
    hope 11
(7) Help child establish new
    activities and hobbies 174

40. CHILD VIOLENT--PARENTS
    WANT HELP

Alternative solutions:

(1) Ask child to move out 156
(2) Talk to a professional
    counselor 13
(3) Talk to a physician 82
(4) Call the police 95
(5) Talk to family and friends
    for advice 51
(6) Ignore the problem, wait and
    hope 11
(7) Talk to minister, priest, or
    rabbi for help 89
(8) Threaten person involved . . .155
(9) Call local crisis hot-line . .173

41. CHILD ABUSE--BY NEIGHBOR

Alternative solutions:

(1) Call the police 95
(2) Report it to welfare
    department 98
(3) Talk to neighbor 99
(4) Ignore the problem, wait and
    hope 11
(5) Talk to a professional
    counselor 13
(6) Write an unsigned letter to
    neighbor 27
(7) Call local crisis hot-line . .173
(8) Threaten person involved . . .155

42. CHILD ABUSE--BY SPOUSE

Alternative solutions:

(1) Call the police 95
(2) Report it to welfare
    department 98
(3) Run away from home 88
(4) Talk to professional
    counselor 13
(5) Talk to family and friends
    for advice 51
(6) Call local crisis hot-line . .173
(7) Ignore the problem, wait and
    hope 11
(8) Ask parent, spouse, or child
    to leave the home 83

43. CHILD CARE--NEEDS CHILD
    CARE SERVICES

See: "OCCUPATION PROBLEMS"

      Child care--Needs child care

44. CHILD SUPPORT PROBLEMS

See: "FINANCIAL PROBLEMS"

Child support problems

45. DEATH--OF PARENT OR SPOUSE CAUSING EMOTIONAL PROBLEMS

Alternative solutions:

(1) Talk to minister, priest, or rabbi for help 89
(2) Talk to a professional counselor 13
(3) Ignore the problem, wait and hope 11
(4) Call local crisis hot-line . . .173

46. DEATH--OF PARENT OR SPOUSE CAUSING FINANCIAL PROBLEMS

See: "FINANCIAL PROBLEMS"

Death of parent or spouse causing financial problems

47. DISCIPLINE--PROBLEM DISCIPLINING CHILD

Alternative solutions:

(1) Talk to family and friends for advice 51
(2) Go to public library for information 12
(3) Talk to a professional counselor 13
(4) Talk to the teacher 41
(5) Talk to school psychologist . . 42
(6) Attend class to learn parenting skills 93
(7) Ask child to move out 156

48. DIVORCE--EMOTIONAL PROBLEMS IN ONE SPOUSE

Alternative solutions:

(1) Ignore the problem, wait and hope 11
(2) Talk to minister, priest, or rabbi for help 89
(3) Talk to a professional counselor 13

49. DIVORCE--CAUSING FINANCIAL PROBLEMS

See: "FINANCIAL PROBLEMS"

Divorce--Causing financial problems

50. DIVORCE--WANTS HELP DECIDING ABOUT GETTING DIVORCED

Alternative solutions:

(1) Obtain legal assistance 9
(2) Talk to minister, priest, or rabbi for help 89
(3) Talk to a professional counselor 13
(4) Talk to family and friends for advice 51
(5) Live separately from spouse . . 91

51. DRUGS--CHILD ABUSES DRUGS

See: "FAMILY AND FRIENDS"

Alcohol--Child abuses alcohol

52. DRUGS--PARENT ABUSES DRUGS

See: "FAMILY AND FRIENDS"

Alcohol--Parent abuses alcohol

53. DRUGS--SPOUSE ABUSES DRUGS

See: "FAMILY AND FRIENDS"

Alcohol--Spouse abuses alcohol

54. ILLEGITIMATE CHILD--CAUSING EMOTIONAL PROBLEMS IN MOTHER OR CHILD

Alternative solutions:

(1) Ignore the problem, wait and hope 11
(2) Talk to a professional counselor 13
(3) Talk to minister, priest, or rabbi for help 89

55. ILLEGITIMATE CHILD--CAUSING FINANCIAL PROBLEMS

See: "FINANCIAL PROBLEMS"

Illegitimate child causing financial problems

56. INJURY--TO FAMILY MEMBER CAUSING EMOTIONAL PROBLEMS TO INJURED MEMBER

Alternative solutions:

(1) Talk to a professional counselor 13
(2) Talk to a physician 82

(3) Talk to minister, priest, or
    rabbi for help 89
(4) Ignore the problem, wait and
    hope 11
(5) Talk to state agency for the
    handicapped 94
(6) See if city or county provides
    services 37

57. INJURY--TO FAMILY MEMBER CAUSING FAMILY FINANCIAL PROBLEMS

See: "FINANCIAL PROBLEMS"

Injury to family member
causing family financial
problems

58. INJURY--TO FAMILY MEMBER CAUSING EMOTIONAL PROBLEMS TO NON-INJURED MEMBERS

Alternative solutions:

(1) Talk to a physician 82
(2) Ignore the problem, wait and
    hope 11
(3) Talk to minister, priest, or
    rabbi for help 89
(4) Talk to a professional
    counselor 13

59. IN-LAWS--INTERFERING

See: "FAMILY AND FRIENDS"

Parents interfering

60. JOB--FAMILY MEMBER UNABLE TO FIND WORK

See: "OCCUPATIONAL PROBLEMS"

Job--Needs a job

61. LEAVE HOME--FOR CHILD WHO WANTS TO LEAVE HOME

Alternative solutions:

(1) Run away from home 88
(2) Talk to family about the
    problem 47
(3) Talk to the teacher about the
    problems at home 41
(4) Talk to a professional
    counselor 13
(5) Talk to school psychologist . . 42
(6) Call the local churches 63
(7) See if city or county provides
    services 37

62. MARITAL PROBLEMS--UNHAPPY IN MARRIAGE

Alternative solutions:

(1) Talk to a professional
    counselor 13
(2) Live separately from spouse . . 91
(3) Get a divorce 102
(4) Talk to minister, priest, or
    rabbi for help 89
(5) Ignore the problem, wait and
    hope 11
(6) Arrange activities for
    yourself 90
(7) Set aside time to be together .100

63. MARRIAGE--WANTS HELP DECIDING ABOUT GETTING MARRIED

Alternative solutions:

(1) Live with person 92
(2) Talk to a professional
    counselor 13
(3) Talk to minister, priest, or
    rabbi for help 89
(4) Talk to family and friends
    for advice 51

64. MARRIAGE FALLING APART

Alternative solutions:

(1) Set aside time to be together .100
(2) Talk to a professional
    counselor 13
(3) Talk to minister, priest, or
    rabbi for help 89
(4) Arrange activities for
    yourself 90
(5) Ignore the problem, wait and
    hope 11

65. PARENT--AGING PARENT NEEDS CARE

Alternative solutions:

(1) Move parent to your home . . . 76
(2) Ask relative to take parent
    into his or her home 77
(3) Pay someone to live with
    parent 78
(4) Place parent in a nursing
    home 79
(5) See if city or county provides
    services 37
(6) Hire someone part-time 80
(7) Talk to nursing home
    directors 81

66. PARENTS--CHILD FEELS HE OR SHE
CANNOT TALK ABOUT CERTAIN
PROBLEMS WITH PARENTS

Alternative solutions:

(1) Talk to family and friends
for advice 51
(2) Talk to the teacher 41
(3) Talk to school psychologist . . 42
(4) Call local crisis hot-line . . .173
(5) Talk to a professional
counselor 13
(6) Tell your parents how the
situation is affecting you . . .127

67. PARENTS--CHILD FEELS PARENTS
ARE TOO STRICT OR OLD-FASHIONED

Alternative solutions:

(1) Talk to a professional
counselor 13
(2) Talk to school psychologist . . 42
(3) Talk to the teacher 41
(4) Talk to family member about
the problem 47
(5) Run away from home 88
(6) Ignore the problem, wait and
hope 11
(7) Tell your parents how the
situation is affecting you . . .127

68. PARENTS--CHILD FEELS PARENTS
DON'T UNDERSTAND HIM OR HER

See: "FAMILY AND FRIENDS"

Parents--Child feels parents
are too strict or old-
fashioned

69. PARENTS--FIGHT TOO MUCH

Alternative solutions:

(1) Talk to minister, priest, or
rabbi for help 89
(2) Talk to the teacher 41
(3) Run away from home 88
(4) Talk to family member about
the problem 47
(5) Call local crisis hot-line . . .173
(6) Talk to family and friends
for advice 51
(7) Talk to a professional
counselor 13
(8) Tell your parents how the
situation is affecting you . . .127
(9) Call the police 95

70. PARENTS--INTERFERING

Alternative solutions:

(1) Tell your parents how the
situation is affecting you . . .127
(2) Talk to family member about
the problem 47
(3) Ignore the problem, wait and
hope 11
(4) Talk to a professional
counselor 13
(5) Threaten person involved 155

71. PREGNANT DAUGHTER--SCHOOL
PROBLEMS

See: "EDUCATION PROBLEMS"

Pregnant student--Problems
in school

72. RETARDED CHILD--PROBLEMS RAISING
RETARDED CHILD

Alternative solutions:

(1) Talk to the teacher 41
(2) Talk to state agency for the
handicapped 94
(3) Arrange child care 1
(4) Talk to a physician 82
(5) See if city or county provides
services 37
(6) Go to public library for
information 12
(7) Find a tutor 46

73. RUNAWAY--CHILD HAS RUN AWAY

Alternative solutions:

(1) Contact places 84
(2) Talk to a professional
counselor 13
(3) Ignore the problem, wait and
hope 11
(4) Call the police 95
(5) Call the local crisis hot-line .173

74. RUNAWAY--CHILD THREATENS TO
RUN AWAY

Alternative solutions:

(1) Ignore the problem, wait and
hope 11
(2) Threaten person involved 155
(3) Ask parent, spouse, or child
to leave the home 83

(4) Talk to a professional
    counselor 13
(5) Attend class to learn
    parenting skills 93
(6) Talk to minister, priest, or
    rabbi for help 89
(7) Set aside time to be together .100

75. SENILE ADULT

See: "FAMILY AND FRIENDS PROBLEMS"

      Aging parent needs care

76. SEPARATION--CAUSING FINANCIAL
    PROBLEMS

See: "FINANCIAL PROBLEMS"

      Separation--Causing
      financial problems

77. SEPARATION--EMOTIONAL PROBLEMS
    IN ONE SPOUSE

See: "FAMILY AND FRIENDS PROBLEMS"

      Divorce--Emotional problems
      in one spouse

78. SEPARATION--WANTS HELP DECIDING
    ABOUT GETTING SEPARATED

Alternative solutions:

(1) Talk to a professional
    counselor 13
(2) Talk to minister, priest, or
    rabbi for help 89
(3) Obtain legal assistance 9
(4) Talk to family and friends
    for advice 51
(5) Live separately from spouse . . 91

79. SPOUSE--DOESN'T HELP ENOUGH
    WITH HOME

Alternative solutions:

(1) Tell your spouse how the
    situation is affecting you . .127
(2) Hire someone to do the
    housework 2
(3) Talk to a professional
    counselor 13
(4) Ignore the problem, wait and
    hope 11
(5) Run away from home 88

80. SPOUSE--FEELS SPOUSE IS NOT
    HOME ENOUGH

Alternative solutions:

(1) Talk to family member about
    problem 47
(2) Arrange activities for
    yourself 90
(3) Talk to a professional
    counselor 13
(4) Set aside time to be together .100
(5) Complain 166

81. SPOUSES--FIGHTING OVER CHILD
    REARING

Alternative solutions:

(1) Arrange child care 1
(2) Talk to a professional
    counselor 13
(3) Talk to minister, priest, or
    rabbi for help 89
(4) Live separately from spouse . . 91
(5) Ignore the problem, wait and
    hope 11
(6) Attend class to learn parent-
    ing skills 93
(7) Hire a baby sitter 73

82. SPOUSES--FIGHTING OVER MONEY

Alternative solutions:

(1) Obtain financial public
    assistance in meantime 85
(2) Live separately from spouse . . 91
(3) Call local crisis hot-line . .173
(4) Go to public library for
    information 12
(5) Ignore the problem, wait and
    hope 11
(6) You obtain job to ease
    financial situation 103
(7) Talk to a professional
    counselor 13
(8) Talk to minister, priest, or
    rabbi for help 89

83. SPOUSE NOT HELPING ENOUGH
    WITH CHILD REARING

Alternative solutions:

(1) Tell you spouse how the
    situation is affecting you . .127

(2) Arrange child care 1
(3) Talk to a professional
    counselor 13
(4) Ignore the problem, wait and
    hope 11
(5) Ask parent, spouse, or child
    to leave the home 83
(6) Arrange activities for
    yourself 90
(7) Rearrange finances so you
    don't have to work so hard . . .101

84. SPOUSE VIOLENT--SPOUSE WANTS HELP

Alternative solutions:

(1) Call local crisis hot-line . . .173
(2) Live separately from spouse . . 91
(3) Talk to family and friends
    for advice 51
(4) Call the police 95

(5) Talk to a professional
    counselor 13
(6) Talk to minister, priest, or
    rabbi for help 89
(7) Ignore the problem, wait and
    hope 11
(8) Threaten person involved . . .155

85. WORKING TOO HARD--WORRIED BECAUSE FAMILY MEMBER IS WORKING TOO HARD

Alternative solutions:

(1) Rearrange finances so you
    don't have to work so hard . .101
(2) Talk to a physician 82
(3) You obtain job to ease
    financial situation 103
(4) Talk to a professional
    counselor 13
(5) Set aside time to be together .100

Financial

86. ALIMONY--NOT RECEIVING PAYMENTS

Alternative solutions:

(1) Obtain legal assistance 9
(2) Talk to family member about
    the problem 47
(3) Obtain financial public
    assistance in meantime 85
(4) See if city or county
    provides services 37
(5) Get a loan from friends or
    relatives 108

87. BANKRUPTCY

Alternative solutions:

(1) Obtain legal assistance 9
(2) Talk to banks to obtain loan . .104
(3) Obtain financial public
    assistance in meantime 85
(4) Ignore the problem, wait and
    hope 11
(5) Contact creditors to arrange
    partial payments 176

88. BUDGETING--NEEDS HELP BUDGETING BETTER

Alternative solutions:

(1) Talk to family and friends
    for advice 51
(2) Write down budget and keep
    track of expenses 105
(3) Increase amount of money
    available 106
(4) Call local crisis hot-line . .173
(5) Go to public library for
    information 12

89. CASH--NEEDS MONEY

See: "FINANCIAL PROBLEMS"

    Money--Needs money

90. CHILD SUPPORT PAYMENTS-- NOT RECEIVING

Alternative solutions:

(1) Obtain legal assistance 9

(2) Speak to family member about
    problem 47
(3) Obtain financial public
    assistance in meantime 85
(4) Get a loan from friends or
    relatives 108

91. CLOTHING--NEEDS MONEY FOR

Alternative solutions:

(1) Contact League of Women
    Voters, Red Cross, Salvation
    Army, Council of Churches . . .107
(2) Get a loan from friends or
    relatives 108
(3) Increase amount of money
    available 106
(4) Go to public library for
    information 12

92. DEATH--OF PARENT OR SPOUSE CAUSING FINANCIAL PROBLEMS

Alternative solutions:

(1) Get a loan from friends or
    relatives 108
(2) Talk to banks to obtain loan .104
(3) Obtain financial public
    assistance in meantime 85
(4) Increase amount of money
    available 106
(5) Contact League of Women
    Voters, Red Cross, Salvation
    Army, Council of Churches . . .107

93. DISABLED VETERAN--NEEDS MONEY

Alternative solutions:

(1) Obtain financial public
    assistance in meantime 85
(2) Call Veterans Administration
    for loan or benefits 109
(3) Contact League of Women
    Voters, Red Cross, Salvation
    Army, Council of Churches . . .107
(4) Get a loan from friends or
    relatives 108
(5) Talk to banks to obtain loan .104
(6) Increase amount of money
    available 106
(7) Go to public library for
    information 12

94. DIVORCE--CAUSING FINANCIAL PROBLEMS

Alternative solutions:

(1) Get a loan from friends or
    relatives 108
(2) Talk to banks to obtain loan .104
(3) Obtain financial public
    assistance in meantime 85
(4) Increase amount of money
    available 106
(5) Obtain legal assistance 9

95. ELECTRICITY--NEEDS MONEY FOR

Alternative solutions:

(1) Obtain financial public
    assistance in meantime 85
(2) Contact League of Women
    Voters, Red Cross, Salvation
    Army, Council of Churches . . .107
(3) Go to public library for
    information 12
(4) Get a loan from friends or
    relatives 108
(5) Contact creditors to arrange
    for partial payments 176
(6) Ignore the problem, wait and
    hope 11

96. EDUCATION--NEEDS MONEY TO CONTINUE EDUCATION

Alternative solutions:

(1) Talk to banks to obtain loan .104
(2) Get a loan from school,
    scholarship, or community . . .110
(3) Get a loan from friends or
    relatives 108
(4) Call Veterans Administration
    for loan or benefits 109
(5) Be a part-time student 52

97. FINANCIALLY DEPENDENT-- DOESN'T LIKE IT

Alternative solutions:

(1) Get a full-time job 111
(2) Get a part-time job 112
(3) Obtain financial public
    assistance in meantime 85
(4) Ignore the problem, wait and
    hope 11

98. FOOD--NEEDS MONEY FOR

Alternative solutions:

(1) Obtain Food Stamps 113
(2) Contact League of Women
    Voters, Red Cross, Salvation
    Army, Council of Churches . . .107
(3) Get a loan from friends or
    relatives 108

99. FURNITURE--NEEDS MONEY FOR

Alternative solutions:

(1) Obtain financial public
    assistance in meantime 85
(2) Contact League of Women
    Voters, Red Cross, Salvation
    Army, Council of Churches . . .107
(3) Get a loan from friends or
    relatives 108
(4) Increase amount of money
    available 106
(5) Go to public library for
    information 12
(6) Ignore the problem, wait and
    hope 11
(7) Read ads in newspaper or
    Yellow Pages 142

100. GAS--NEEDS MONEY FOR

See: "FINANCIAL PROBLEMS"

    Electricity--Needs money for

101. HOME IMPROVEMENTS--NEEDS MONEY FOR

Alternative solutions:

(1) Contact League of Women
    Voters, Red Cross, Salvation
    Army, Council of Churches . . .107
(2) Increase amount of money
    available 106
(3) Talk to banks to obtain loan . .104
(4) See if city or county provides
    services 37

102. HOUSING--NEEDS MONEY FOR

Alternative solutions:

(1) Obtain financial public
    assistance in meantime 85
(2) Talk to banks to obtain loan . .104
(3) Get a loan from friends or
    relatives 108

(4) Increase amount of money
    available 106
(5) Contact League of Women
    Voters, Red Cross, Salvation
    Army, Council of Churches . .107
(6) Go to public library for
    information 12
(7) Call Federal Housing
    Authority 135
(8) Call local crisis hot-line .173

103. ILLEGITIMATE CHILD--CAUSING FINANCIAL PROBLEMS

Alternative solutions:

(1) Obtain financial public
    assistance in meantime . . . 85
(2) Obtain Food Stamps 113
(3) Increase amount of money
    available 106
(4) Contact League of Women
    Voters, Red Cross, Salvation
    Army, Council of Churches . .107
(5) Talk to welfare counselor
    for information 126

104. INCOME--NO STEADY INCOME

Alternative solutions:

(1) Get a full-time job 111
(2) Get a part-time job 112
(3) Obtain financial public
    assistance in meantime . . . 85
(4) Be financially dependent
    upon someone else 114
(5) See if city or county
    provides services 37
(6) Go to public library for
    information 12

105. INJURY TO FAMILY MEMBER CAUSING FAMILY FINANCIAL PROBLEMS

Alternative solutions:

(1) Increase amount of money
    available 106
(2) Obtain financial public
    assistance in meantime . . . 85
(3) Check your insurance policy
    for coverage 115
(4) Talk to banks to obtain
    loan 104
(5) Get a loan from friends or
    relatives 108

(6) Talk to state agency for the
    handicapped 94
(7) Talk to Social Security
    Administration 121

106. INSURANCE--NEEDS MONEY FOR

Alternative solutions:

(1) Go to public library for
    information 12
(2) Get a loan from friends or
    relatives 108
(3) Increase amount of money
    available 106

107. JAIL--NEEDS MONEY TO GET SOMEONE OUT OF JAIL

Alternative solutions:

(1) Get a loan from friends or
    relatives 108
(2) Contact League of Women
    Voters, Red Cross, Salvation
    Army, Council of Churches . . .107
(3) Ignore the problem, wait and
    hope 11

108. LEGAL ADVICE--NEEDS MONEY FOR

Alternative solutions:

(1) Get a loan from friends or
    relatives 108
(2) Talk to the Legal Aid Society
    for legal advice 116
(3) Increase amount of money
    available 106
(4) Read ads in newspaper or
    Yellow Pages 142

109. LOAN--NEEDS INFORMATION ABOUT HOW TO GET ONE

Alternative solutions:

(1) Talk to banker or investment
    counselor 119
(2) Go to public library for
    information 12
(3) Talk to family and friends
    for advice 51
(4) Call Federal Housing
    Authority 135

110. LOAN--NEEDS LOAN TO BUY HOME

See: "FINANCIAL PROBLEMS"

       Loan--Needs information
       about how to get one

111. LOAN CONSOLIDATION--NEEDS TO ARRANGE

Alternative solutions:

(1) Talk to banker or investment
    counselor 119
(2) Go to public library for
    information 12
(3) Obtain legal assistance 9
(4) Contact creditors to arrange
    partial payments 176

112. MEDICAL SUPPLIES--NEEDS MONEY FOR

Alternative solutions:

(1) Contact League of Women
    Voters, Red Cross, Salvation
    Army, Council of Churches . . .107
(2) Get a loan from friends or
    relatives 108
(3) Increase amount of money
    available 106
(4) Obtain financial public
    assistance in meantime 85
(5) Ignore the problem, wait and
    hope 11
(6) Talk to public health
    department 97

113. MONEY--NEEDS MONEY

Alternative solutions:

(1) Contact League of Women
    Voters, Red Cross, Salvation
    Army, Council of Churches . . .107
(2) Get a loan from friends or
    relatives 108
(3) Talk to banks to obtain loan .104
(4) Increase amount of money
    available 106
(5) Talk to a welfare counselor
    for information 126

114. MONEY--HAS LESS MONEY THAN FRIENDS

Alternative solutions:

(1) Increase amount of money
    available 106
(2) Obtain financial public
    assistance in meantime 85
(3) Ask for a raise on your job . .118
(4) Change the situation 162
(5) Ignore the problem, wait and
    hope 11

115. MONEY--SPENDING TOO MUCH MONEY

See: "FINANCIAL PROBLEMS"

Budgeting--Needs help
budgeting money

**116. OLD AGE--WORRIED ABOUT
FINANCIAL SECURITY IN OLD AGE**

Alternative solutions:

(1) Talk to banker or
investment counselor 119
(2) Investigate retirement
program where you work 120
(3) Talk to Social Security
Administration 121

117. RENT--NEEDS MONEY FOR

Alternative solutions:

(1) Obtain financial public
assistance in meantime 85
(2) Get a loan from friends or
relatives 108
(3) Contact League of Women
Voters, Red Cross, Salvation
Army, Council of Churches . . .107
(4) Go to public library for
information 12
(5) Increase amount of money
available 106
(6) Ignore the problem, wait and
hope 11
(7) Contact creditors to arrange
partial payments 176

**118. SEPARATION--CAUSING FINANCIAL
PROBLEMS**

Alternative solutions:

(1) Get a loan from friends or
relatives 108
(2) Talk to banks to obtain loan . .104
(3) Obtain financial public
assistance in meantime 85
(4) Increase amount of money
available 106

**119. SOCIAL SECURITY
INSURANCE PROBLEMS**

Alternative solutions:

(1) Call Medicaid, Medicare,
Social Security, or welfare,
and complain 117

(2) Obtain legal assistance 9
(3) Call local crisis hot-line . .173
(4) Talk to welfare counselor for
information 126

120. TAX PROBLEMS

Alternative solutions:

(1) Obtain legal assistance 9
(2) Talk to an accountant 122
(3) Talk to Internal Revenue
Service 123
(4) Talk to family and friends
for advice 51
(5) Go to public library for
information 12

121. TELEPHONE--NEEDS MONEY FOR

Alternative solutions:

(1) Get a loan from friends or
relatives 108
(2) Contact creditors to arrange
partial payments 176
(3) Increase amount of money
available 106
(4) Ignore the problem, wait and
hope 11

**122. TRANSPORTATION--NEEDS
MONEY FOR**

Alternative solutions:

(1) Get a loan from friends or
relatives 108
(2) Contact the League of Women
Voters, Red Cross, Salvation
Army, Council of Churches . . .107
(3) Obtain financial public
assistance in meantime 85
(4) Increase amount of money
available 106

**123. UNEMPLOYMENT COMPENSATION--
LATE OR DENIED**

See: "FINANCIAL PROBLEMS"

Workmen's Compensation--
Late or denied

**124. VETERAN--WANTS TO GET
VETERAN'S BENEFITS**

Alternative solutions:

(1) Call Veterans Administration
for loan or benefits 109

(2) Contact the League of Women
    Voters, Red Cross, Salvation
    Army, Council of Churches . . .107
(3) See if city or county
    provides services 37

125. WATER--NEEDS MONEY FOR

See: "FINANCIAL PROBLEMS"

      Electricity--Needs money for

126. WELFARE--DECIDING WHETHER
     OR NOT TO GET A JOB

Alternative solutions:

(1) Take job and risk the Welfare
    Department's finding out . . .124
(2) Ignore the problem, wait and
    hope 11
(3) Get a loan from friends or
    relatives 108
(4) Talk to welfare counselor for
    information 126

127. WELFARE--DELAYS IN
     RECEIVING CHECKS

Alternative solutions:

(1) Call Medicaid, Medicare,
    Social Security, or Welfare
    and complain 117
(2) Get a loan from friends or
    relatives 108
(3) Obtain legal assistance 9
(4) Write to your Congressperson .125
(5) Talk to a welfare counselor
    for information 126
(6) Threaten person involved . . .155
(7) Go to public library for
    information 12

128. WELFARE--WANTS ADJUSTMENT
     IN WELFARE ALLOWANCE

Alternative solutions:

(1) Call Medicaid, Medicare,
    Social Security, or Welfare,
    and complain 117
(2) Increase amount of money
    available 106
(3) Write to your Congressperson . .125
(4) Talk to welfare counselor for
    information 126

129. WELFARE--WHETHER OR NOT
     TO APPLY FOR

Alternative solutions:

(1) Talk to welfare counselor for
    information 126
(2) Talk to family and friends for
    advice 51
(3) Get a full-time job 111
(4) Go to public library for
    information 12

130. WORKMEN'S COMPENSATION--
     LATE OR DENIED

Alternative solutions:

(1) Talk to the Legal Aid Society
    for advice 116
(2) Obtain financial public
    assistance in meantime 85
(3) Talk to banks to obtain loan . .104
(4) Be financially dependent on
    someone else 114
(5) Write to your Congressperson . .125
(6) Contact state employment
    office to see what caused this
    problem and what you should do
    to straighten things out 23

Health

131. ABORTION--NEEDS INFORMATION

Alternative solutions:

(1) Talk to a physician 82
(2) Talk to Planned Parenthood . . 96
(3) Talk to Public Health
    Department 97

(4) Talk to a professional
    counselor 13
(5) Talk to family and friends
    for advice 51
(6) Call local crisis hot-line . . .173
(7) Go to public library for
    information 12

132. ACHES

Alternative solutions:

(1) Talk to a physician 82
(2) Ignore the problem, wait and
    hope 11
(3) Talk to Public Health
    Department 97
(4) Talk to pharmacist for
    suggestions 128

133. ALCOHOL--RELATED PROBLEMS

Alternative solutions:

(1) Talk to a physician 82
(2) Talk to Public Health
    Department 97
(3) Ignore the problem, wait and
    hope 11
(4) Call Alcoholics Anonymous . . .129
(5) Talk to pharmacist for
    suggestions 128
(6) Check into a hospital for
    treatment 130

134. ALLERGY PROBLEMS

Alternative solutions:

(1) Talk to a physician 82
(2) Talk to Public Health
    Department 97
(3) Ignore the problem, wait and
    hope 11
(4) Talk to pharmacist for
    suggestions 128
(5) Check into a hospital for
    treatment 130

135. ANXIETY PROBLEMS

Alternative solutions:

(1) Talk to a professional
    counselor 13
(2) Talk to a physician 82
(3) Talk to pharmacist for
    suggestions 128
(4) Ignore the problem, wait and
    hope 11
(5) Go to public library for
    information 12
(6) Try different things and see
    which you like best 163

136. APPETITE PROBLEMS

Alternative solutions:

(1) Talk to a physician 82
(2) Talk to Public Health
    Department 97
(3) Talk to pharmacist for
    suggestions 128
(4) Ignore the problem, wait and
    hope 11

137. BIRTH CONTROL--NEEDS
     INFORMATION

Alternative solutions:

(1) Talk to a physician 82
(2) Talk to Public Health
    Department 97
(3) Talk to Planned Parenthood . . 96
(4) Go to public library for
    information 12
(5) Talk to family and friends
    for advice 51
(6) Talk to a school nurse 74

138. DEPRESSION

Alternative solutions:

(1) Talk to a professional
    counselor 13
(2) Talk to a physician 82
(3) Ignore the problem, wait and
    hope 11
(4) Check into a hospital for
    treatment 130
(5) Talk to school psychologist . . 42
(6) Go to public library for
    information 12
(7) Try different things and see
    which you like best 163
(8) Become a volunteer in a
    community service agency . . .175
(9) Call local crisis hot-line . .173

139. DIZZINESS

Alternative solutions:

(1) Talk to a physician 82
(2) Talk to Public Health
    Department 97
(3) Ignore the problem, wait and
    hope 11
(4) Check into a hospital for
    treatment 130

140. DRUG–RELATED PROBLEMS

Alternative solutions:

(1) Talk to a physician 82
(2) Talk to Public Health
    Department 97
(3) Ignore the problem, wait and
    hope 11
(4) Check into a hospital for
    treatment 130
(5) Call local crisis hot-line . .173
(6) Talk to pharmacist for
    suggestions 128

141. EYE TROUBLE

Alternative solutions:

(1) Talk to a physician 82
(2) Talk to Public Health
    Department 97
(3) Talk to pharmacist for
    suggestions 128
(4) Ignore the problem, wait and
    hope 11

142. HEADACHES

Alternative solutions:

(1) Talk to a physician 82
(2) Talk to Public Health
    Department 97
(3) Talk to pharmacist for
    suggestions 128
(4) Ignore the problem, wait and
    hope 11

143. HEART TROUBLE

Alternative solutions:

(1) Talk to a physician 82
(2) Talk to Public Health
    Department 97
(3) Ignore the problem, wait and
    hope 11
(4) Check into a hospital for
    treatment 130
(5) Go to public library for
    information 12

144. HIGH BLOOD PRESSURE

Alternative solutions:

(1) Talk to a physician 82
(2) Talk to Public Health
    Department 97

(3) Check into a hospital for
    treatment 130
(4) Ignore the problem, wait and
    hope 11
(5) Go to public library for
    information 12

145. INJURY--CAUSING EMOTIONAL PROBLEMS

See: "FAMILY AND FRIENDS PROBLEMS"

Injury--Causing emotional
problems

146. INSANE--THOUGHTS OF GOING INSANE

Alternative solutions:

(1) Check into a hospital for
    treatment 130
(2) Talk to a professional
    counselor 13
(3) Talk to a physician 82
(4) Talk to Public Health
    Department 97
(5) Ignore the problem, wait and
    hope 11
(6) Call local crisis hot-line . .173

147. MEDICAID--NOT RECEIVING SERVICE

Alternative solutions:

(1) Call Medicaid, Medicare,
    Social Security, or Welfare,
    and complain 117
(2) Obtain legal assistance 9
(3) Ignore the problem, wait and
    hope 11
(4) Talk to a physician 82
(5) Talk to Public Health
    Department 97

148. MEDICAL SUPPLIES--NEEDS MONEY FOR

See: "FINANCIAL PROBLEMS"

Medical supplies--needs
money for

149. MEDICARE--NOT RECEIVING SERVICE

Alternative solutions:

(1) Call Medicaid, Medicare,
    Social Security, or Welfare,
    and complain 117

(2) Obtain legal assistance 9
(3) Ignore the problem, wait and
hope 11
(4) Talk to a physician 82
(5) Talk to Public Health
Department 97

150. MEMORY IS POOR

Alternative solutions:

(1) Talk to a physician 82
(2) Talk to Public Health
Department 97
(3) Check into a hospital for
treatment 130
(4) Ignore the problem, wait and
hope 11
(5) Go to public library for
information 12

151. MENSTRUATION PROBLEMS

Alternative solutions:

(1) Talk to a physician 82
(2) Talk to Public Health
Department 97
(3) Talk to pharmacist for
suggestions 128
(4) Ignore the problem, wait and
hope 11
(5) Go to public library for
information 12

152. NERVOUSNESS

See: "HEALTH PROBLEMS"

Anxiety problems

153. OVERWEIGHT

See: "SELF-IMPROVEMENT PROBLEMS"

Overweight

154. PHYSICAL PAINS

Alternative solutions:

(1) Talk to a physician 82
(2) Go to Public Health
Department 97
(3) Talk to pharmacist for
suggestions 128
(4) Check into a hospital for
treatment 130
(5) Ignore the problem, wait and
hope 11

155. PREGNANCY--NEEDS MEDICAL CARE

Alternative solutions:

(1) Talk to a physician 82
(2) Talk to Public Health
Department 97
(3) Go to well-baby clinic 131
(4) Call Obstetrics Department
in hospital 132
(5) Ignore the problem, wait and
hope 11

156. PREGNANCY--NEEDS PREGNANCY TEST

Alternative solutions:

(1) Talk to a physician 82
(2) Talk to Public Health
Department 97
(3) Talk to Planned Parenthood . . 96
(4) Talk to a school nurse 74

157. RAPE--CAUSING EMOTIONAL PROBLEMS

Alternative solutions:

(1) Talk to a physician 82
(2) Talk to a professional
counselor 13
(3) Talk to rape center counselor .133
(4) Talk to family and friends
for advice 51
(5) Call local crisis hot-line . .173
(6) Talk to school psychologist . . 42

158. RAPE--CAUSING PHYSICAL PROBLEMS

Alternative solutions:

(1) Talk to a physician 82
(2) Talk to Public Health
Department 97
(3) Talk to pharmacist for
suggestions 128
(4) Check into a hospital for
treatment 130
(5) Ignore the problem, wait and
hope 11
(6) Talk to rape center counselor .133

159. SEXUAL PROBLEMS

Alternative solutions:

(1) Talk to a physician 82
(2) Talk to a professional
counselor 13

(3) Talk to a sex therapist 134
(4) Go to public library for
    information 12
(5) Ignore the problem, wait and
    hope 11

160. SLEEPING PROBLEMS

Alternative solutions:

(1) Talk to a physician 82
(2) Talk to Public Health
    Department 97
(3) Talk to pharmacist for
    suggestions 128
(4) Check into a hospital for
    treatment 130
(5) Go to public library for
    information 12
(6) Ignore the problem, wait and
    hope 11

161. STOMACH PROBLEMS

Alternative solutions:

(1) Talk to a physician 82
(2) Talk to Public Health
    Department 97
(3) Talk to pharmacist for
    suggestions 128
(4) Check into a hospital for
    treatment 130
(5) Ignore the problem, wait and
    hope 11

162. SUICIDAL THOUGHTS OR ATTEMPTS

Alternative solutions:

(1) Talk to a professional
    counselor 13
(2) Talk to a physician 82
(3) Check into a hospital for
    treatment 130
(4) Call local crisis hot-line . .173
(5) Talk to Public Health
    Department 97
(6) Talk with minister, priest, or
    rabbi for help 89
(7) Try different things and see
    which you like best 163

163. TIRED TOO MUCH OF THE TIME

Alternative solutions:

(1) Talk to a physician 82
(2) Talk to Public Health
    Department 97
(3) Talk to pharmacist for
    suggestions 128
(4) Check into a hospital for
    treatment 130
(5) Ignore the problem, wait and
    hope 11

164. TOBACCO--RELATED PROBLEMS

Alternative solutions:

(1) Talk to a physician 82
(2) Talk to Public Health
    Department 97
(3) Check into a hospital for
    treatment 130
(4) Talk to pharmacist for
    suggestions 128
(5) Ignore the problem, wait and
    hope 11

165. UNDERWEIGHT

See: "SELF-IMPROVEMENT PROBLEMS"

       Underweight

166. VENEREAL DISEASE

Alternative solutions:

(1) Talk to a physician 82
(2) Talk to Public Health
    Department 97
(3) Check into a hospital for
    treatment 130
(4) Talk to a school nurse 74
(5) Go to public library for
    information 12

167. WORRY--WORRY BECOMING A
     HEALTH PROBLEM

See: "HEALTH PROBLEMS"

       Anxiety Problems

Housing

168. ELECTRICITY--NEEDS MONEY FOR

See: "FINANCIAL PROBLEMS"

Electricity--Needs money for

169. EVICTION NOTICE

A. If due to failure to pay rent:

See: "FINANCIAL PROBLEMS"

Rent--Needs money
for rent

B. If not due to failure to pay rent:

170. FURNITURE--NEEDS MONEY FOR

See: "FINANCIAL PROBLEMS"

Furniture--Needs money for

171. GAS OFF--NEEDS MONEY FOR

See: "FINANCIAL PROBLEMS"

Gas--Needs money for

172. HOME IMPROVEMENT--NEEDS HELP TO DO

Alternative solutions:

173. HOME IMPROVEMENT--NEEDS MONEY FOR

See: "FINANCIAL PROBLEMS"

Home Improvement--Needs
money for

174. HOUSING--NEEDS A PLACE TO LIVE

Alternative solutions:

175. HOUSING--NEEDS PLACE TO STAY TEMPORARILY

Alternative solutions:

176. HOUSING--POOR HOUSING CONDITIONS

Alternative solutions:

177. HOUSING--WANTS TO BUY HOME

Alternative solutions:

(2) Talk to family and friends
for advice 51
(3) Talk to area real estate
agents 151
(4) Go up and down streets looking
for "For Rent" and "For Sale"
signs 145

178. HOUSING--WANTS TO RENT

Alternative solutions:

(1) Read "For Rent" or "For Sale"
ads in newspaper 144
(2) Talk to family and friends
for advice 51
(3) Talk to area real estate
agents 151
(4) Go up and down streets looking
for "For Rent" and "For Sale"
signs 145
(5) Call landlords and see if they
have anything open 146

179. LANDLORD--RAISED RENT

Alternative solutions:

(1) Find a new place to live 136
(2) Speak to Tenant's Rights
Association 139
(3) Talk to landlord 138
(4) Obtain legal assistance 9

180. LANDLORD--TENANT WANTS TO BREAK LEASE

Alternative solutions:

(1) Talk to landlord 138
(2) Speak to Tenant's Rights
Association 139
(3) Obtain legal assistance 9
(4) Talk to family and friends
for advice 51
(5) Put an ad in the newspaper
for help 141

181. LANDLORD--WANTS TO SELL HOUSE

Alternative solutions:

(1) Find a new place to live 136
(2) Talk to landlord 138
(3) Buy house from landlord 152
(4) Speak to Tenant's Rights
Association 139

182. LANDLORD--WON'T MAKE REPAIRS

See: "HOUSING PROBLEMS"

Housing--Poor conditions

183. LIVING WITH RELATIVES-- CAUSING PROBLEMS

Alternative solutions:

(1) Find a new place to live 136
(2) Find a different place to stay
temporarily 153
(3) Move in with relatives or
friends 137
(4) Tell your relatives about how
the situation is affecting you .127
(5) Run away from home 88

184. LOAN--NEEDS LOAN TO BUY HOME

See: "FINANCIAL PROBLEMS"

Loan--Needs loan to buy home

185. MONEY--NEEDS MONEY FOR HOUSING

See: "FINANCIAL PROBLEMS"

Housing--Needs money for

186. PRIVACY--LACKING PRIVACY IN LIVING SITUATION

See: "HOUSING PROBLEMS"

Living with relatives--
Causing problems

187. RENT--NEEDS MONEY FOR

See: "FINANCIAL PROBLEMS"

Rent--Needs money for rent

188. TELEPHONE--NEEDS MONEY FOR

See: "FINANCIAL PROBLEMS"

Telephone--Needs money for

189. UNDESIRABLE LOCATION--LIVING IN UNDESIRABLE NEIGHBORHOOD

A. If tenant wants to find
different place to live, see:

"HOUSING PROBLEMS" -- Needs
place to stay

"HOUSING PROBLEMS" -- Wants
to buy

"HOUSING PROBLEMS" -- Wants
to rent

B.   If tenant does not want to move:

(1) Ignore the problem, wait and
hope 11

(2) Have home moved 154

190. WATER--NEEDS MONEY FOR

See: "FINANCIAL PROBLEMS"

Electricity--needs money for

Occupation

191. CHILD CARE--NEEDED WHILE
WORKING

Alternative solutions:

(1) Find day care facility 70
(2) Put child in nursery school . . 71
(3) Ask friend or relative to
care for child 72
(4) Hire a baby sitter 73
(5) Talk to family and friends
for advice 51

192. COMBINING HOUSEWORK, CHILDREN
AND JOB

Alternative solutions:

(1) Arrange child care 1
(2) Hire someone to do the
housework 2
(3) Rearrange work hours 3
(4) Change to part-time job 4
(5) Quit job 5

193. GRADUATED--UNSURE WHAT TO
DO NEXT

See: "EDUCATION PROBLEMS"

Graduated--Unsure what to
do next

194. JOB--NO ADVANCEMENT ON
PRESENT JOB

Alternative solutions:

(1) Find a new job 6
(2) Transfer job with same
employer 10
(3) Talk to employer about problem . 7
(4) Complain 166

195. JOB--DISCRIMINATION PROBLEM
ON JOB

Alternative solutions:

(1) Find a new job 6
(2) Talk to employer about
problem 7
(3) Talk to people who are
discriminating 8
(4) Obtain legal assistance 9
(5) Transfer job with same
employer 10
(6) Ignore the problem, wait and
hope 11
(7) See if city or county provides
services 37
(8) Threaten person involved . . .155
(9) Call the local Equal Employment Opportunity office 157

196. JOB--DISSATISFIED WITH
PRESENT JOB

Alternative solutions:

(1) Transfer job with same
employer 10
(2) Find a new job 6
(3) Ignore the problem, wait and
hope 11

197. JOB--DOESN'T KNOW HOW TO
FIND A JOB

See: "OCCUPATION PROBLEMS"

Job--Needs a job

198. JOB--DOESN'T KNOW WHAT
KIND TO DO

Alternative solutions:

(1) Go to public library for
information 12

(2) Talk to a professional
counselor 13
(3) Find a job, and see if you
like the work 14
(4) Talk to working people 15

199. JOB--FIRED FROM JOB

See: "OCCUPATION PROBLEMS"

Job--Needs a job

200. JOB--NEEDS INFORMATION
ABOUT JOB OPENINGS

See: "OCCUPATION PROBLEMS"

Job--Needs a job

201. JOB--WANTS INFORMATION
ABOUT SPECIFIC JOBS

Alternative solutions:

(1) Go to public library for
information 12
(2) Talk to working people 15
(3) Talk to a professional
counselor 13
(4) Contact state employment,
school placement, and Veterans
Administration offices 23

202. JOB--LACKS TRAINING OR
EXPERIENCE

Alternative solutions:

(1) Ask for on-the-job training . . 16
(2) Go to school 17
(3) Find different job to gain
experience 18
(4) Find different job, and go to
school part-time 19
(5) Take different position with
desired employer 20

203. JOB--MAY LOSE JOB

Alternative solutions:

(1) Find a new job 6
(2) Correct problem at present
job 21
(3) Ignore the problem, wait and
hope 11

204. JOB--NEEDS A JOB

Alternative solutions:

(1) Apply from newspaper want ads . 22
(2) Contact state employment,
school placement, and Veterans
Administration offices 23
(3) Contact private employment
agencies 24
(4) Ask friends for help finding
a job 25
(5) Ask previous employers for
job 26
(6) Obtain financial public
assistance in meantime 85
(7) Go to school 17
(8) Talk to a professional
counselor 13

205. JOB--HAS POOR WORK HISTORY,
BUT NEEDS JOB

See: "OCCUPATION PROBLEMS"

Job--Needs a job

206. JOB--TRANSPORTATION PROBLEM
TO WORK

Alternative solutions:

(1) Find public transportation . . 31
(2) Buy a car 32
(3) Rent a car 33
(4) Use a cab 34
(5) Use a bicycle 35
(6) Find someone who would drive
you 36
(7) See if city or county provides
services 37

207. MILITARY--WANTS INFORMATION
ABOUT MILITARY

Alternative solutions:

(1) Call local recruiter 38
(2) Talk to working people 15
(3) Talk to a professional
counselor 13
(4) Go to public library for
information 12

208. OWN BUSINESS--WANTS OWN
     BUSINESS

Alternative solutions:

(1) Contact small business bureau
    and banks 39
(2) Ask business owners for
    suggestions 40
(3) Go to public library for
    information 12

209. PART-TIME JOB--WANTS ONE

See: "OCCUPATION PROBLEMS"

     Job--Needs a job

210. REFUSES TO WORK--FAMILY
     MEMBER REFUSING

Alternative solutions:

(1) Obtain financial public
    assistance in meantime 85
(2) Increase amount of money
    available 106
(3) Threaten person involved . . .155
(4) Talk to a professional
    counselor 13
(5) Talk to family and friends
    for advice 51

(6) Ignore the problem, wait and
    hope 11
(7) Tell the family member how the
    situation is affecting you . . .127
(8) Ask parent, spouse, or child
    to leave the home 83

211. SHIFT CHANGED--CAUSED PROBLEMS
     AT HOME

Alternative solutions:

(1) Arrange to go back on
    original shift 28
(2) Find a new job 6
(3) Correct problems at home . . . 29
(4) Complain 166

212. SUPERVISOR--PROBLEMS AT WORK

Alternative solutions:

(1) Ask to change supervisor . . . 30
(2) Change jobs 6
(3) Ignore the problem, wait and
    hope 11
(4) Talk to employer about problem . 7

213. TRADE--WANTS TO LEARN A TRADE

See: "EDUCATION PROBLEMS"

     Trade--Wants to learn a trade

Self-Improvement

214. ALONE TOO MUCH

See: "SELF-IMPROVEMENT PROBLEMS"

     Lonely

215. ANGER PROBLEM--HARD TO
     HANDLE ANGER

Alternative solutions:

(1) Talk to a professional
    counselor 13
(2) Ignore the problem, wait and
    hope 11
(3) Talk to family and friends
    for advice 51
(4) Talk to a physician 82
(5) Talk to minister, priest, or
    rabbi for help 89

216. APPEARANCE--WANTS TO IMPROVE
     APPEARANCE

Alternative solutions:

(1) Talk to cosmetologist 158
(2) Join Weight Watchers 159
(3) Get more exercise 160
(4) Talk to family and friends
    for advice 51
(5) Talk to a physician 82

217. CONVERSATIONS--TROUBLE TALKING
     TO PEOPLE

Alternative solutions:

(1) Talk to a professional
    counselor 13
(2) Talk to minister, priest, or
    rabbi for help 89

(3) Talk to family and friends
    for advice 51
(4) Make yourself do whatever is
    necessary in hopes of solving
    your problem that way 161
(5) Call local crisis hot-line . . .173
(6) Go to public library for
    information 12

218. DECISIONS--HAS DIFFICULTY MAKING DECISIONS

Alternative solutions:

(1) Talk to a professional
    counselor 13
(2) Talk to minister, priest, or
    rabbi for help 89
(3) Talk to family and friends
    for advice 51
(4) Change the situation 162
(5) Go to public library for
    information 12
(6) Call local crisis hot-line . . .173

219. DEPRESSED

See: "HEALTH PROBLEMS"

      Depressed

220. DISAPPOINTED IN SELF

Alternative solutions:

(1) Talk to a professional
    counselor 13
(2) Talk to minister, priest, or
    rabbi for help 89
(3) Make yourself do whatever is
    necessary in hopes of solving
    your problem that way 161
(4) Change the situation 162

221. DISLIKING SOMEONE

Alternative solutions:

(1) Ignore the problem, wait and
    hope 11
(2) Talk to family and friends
    for advice 51
(3) Talk to minister, priest, or
    rabbi for help 89
(4) Talk to a professional
    counselor 13
(5) Go to public library for
    information 12
(6) Make appointment at county
    mental health clinic 167

222. DISLIKED BY SOMEONE

See: "SELF-IMPROVEMENT PROBLEMS"

      Disliking someone

223. FAILING--AFRAID OF

Alternative solutions:

(1) Talk to a professional
    counselor 13
(2) Talk to minister, priest, or
    rabbi for help 89
(3) Change your situation 162
(4) Make yourself do whatever is
    necessary in hopes of solving
    your problem that way 161
(5) Talk to family and friends
    for advice 51
(6) Become a volunteer in a
    community service agency . . .175
(7) Try different things and see
    which you like best 163

224. FRIENDS--UNABLE TO MAKE FRIENDS

Alternative solutions:

(1) Talk to a professional
    counselor 13
(2) Talk to minister, priest, or
    rabbi for help 89
(3) Make yourself do whatever is
    necessary in hopes of solving
    your problem that way 161
(4) Talk to family and friends
    for advice 51
(5) Try different things and see
    which you like best 163
(6) Become a volunteer in a
    community service agency . . .175

225. GRADUATE EQUIVALENCY DIPLOMA-- WANTS TO OBTAIN

See: "EDUCATION PROBLEMS"

      Graduate Equivalency Diploma

226. HABIT--WANTS TO BREAK A HABIT

Alternative solutions:

(1) Talk to a professional
    counselor 13
(2) Talk to family and friends
    for advice 51

(3) Make yourself do whatever is necessary in hopes of solving your problem that way 161
(4) Change the situation 162

227. HOBBIES

Alternative solutions:

(1) Talk to family and friends for advice 51
(2) Go to public library for information 12
(3) Try different things and see which you like best 163
(4) Go to hobby shop for ideas . . .164
(5) Become a volunteer in a community service agency 175
(6) See if city or county provides services 37

228. INFERIOR--FEELS INFERIOR TO OTHERS

Alternative solutions:

(1) Talk to a professional counselor 13
(2) Talk to minister, priest, or rabbi for help 89
(3) Talk to family and friends for advice 51
(4) Make yourself do whatever is necessary in hopes of solving your problem that way 161
(5) Change the situation 162
(6) Try different things and see which you like best 163
(7) Become a volunteer in a community service agency 175

229. JEALOUS

Alternative solutions:

(1) Talk to a professional counselor 13
(2) Talk to minister, priest, or rabbi for help 89
(3) Talk to family and friends for advice 51
(4) Talk to family member about problem 47
(5) Change the situation 162
(6) Try different things and see which you like best 163

230. LAZY--NOT GETTING ANYTHING DONE

Alternative solutions:

(1) Talk to a professional counselor 13
(2) Talk to minister, priest, or rabbi for help 89
(3) Talk to family and friends for advice 51
(4) Make yourself do whatever is necessary in hopes of solving your problem that way 161

231. LEGAL ADVICE--WANTS TO OBTAIN

Alternative solutions:

(1) Look in the Yellow Pages of the phone book 165
(2) Talk to family and friends for advice 51

232. LONELY

Alternative solutions:

(1) Talk to a professional counselor 13
(2) Talk to minister, priest, or rabbi for help 89
(3) Talk to family and friends for advice 51
(4) Make yourself do whatever is necessary in hopes of solving your problem that way 161
(5) Arrange activities for yourself 90
(6) Become a volunteer in a community service agency 175

233. MADE FUN OF--BEING MADE FUN OF BY OTHERS

Alternative solutions:

(1) Ignore the problem, wait and hope 11
(2) Talk to family member about problem 47
(3) Complain 166
(4) Talk to family and friends for advice 51
(5) Change the situation 162
(6) Talk to a professional counselor 13
(7) Threaten person involved . . .155

234. MARITAL COUNSELING--WANTS
     TO OBTAIN

Alternative solutions:

(1) Make appointment at county
    mental health clinic 167
(2) Look in the Yellow Pages of
    the phone book 165
(3) Talk to family and friends
    for advice 51
(4) Talk to a physician 82
(5) Call local crisis hot-line . . .173
(6) Talk to minister, priest, or
    rabbi for help 89

235. MEDICAL SERVICES--WANTS
     TO OBTAIN

Alternative solutions:

(1) Look in the Yellow Pages of
    the phone book 165
(2) Talk to family and friends
    for advice 51
(3) Talk to a physician 82
(4) Talk to Public Health
    Department 97

236. NERVOUS WITH PEOPLE OF
     OPPOSITE SEX

Alternative solutions:

(1) Talk to a professional
    counselor 13
(2) Talk to minister, priest, or
    rabbi for help 89
(3) Change the situation 162
(4) Make yourself do whatever is
    necessary in hopes of solving
    your problem that way 161
(5) Talk to family and friends
    for advice 51

237. NERVOUS WITH PEOPLE OF SAME SEX

Alternative solutions:

(1) Talk to a professional
    counselor 13
(2) Talk to minister, priest, or
    rabbi for help 89
(3) Change the situation 162
(4) Talk to family and friends
    for advice 51
(5) Make yourself do whatever is
    necessary in hopes of solving
    your problem that way 161

238. NERVOUS--WORRYING TOO MUCH

See: "HEALTH PROBLEMS"

      Anxiety Problems

239. OVERWEIGHT

Alternative solutions:

(1) Talk to a physician 82
(2) Join Weight Watchers 159
(3) Get more exercise 160
(4) Design your own diet or
    follow a formal diet 168
(5) Go to public library for
    information 12
(6) Talk to family and friends
    for advice 51
(7) Talk to a professional
    counselor 13
(8) Talk to pharmacist for
    suggestions 128

240. PROCRASTINATING

See: "SELF-IMPROVEMENT PROBLEMS"

      Lazy--Not getting anything
      done

241. PROFESSIONAL COUNSELING--
     WANTS TO OBTAIN

See: "SELF-IMPROVEMENT PROBLEMS"

      Marital counseling--Wants
      to obtain

242. RECREATION--DOESN'T DO ENOUGH

Alternative solutions:

(1) Join YMCA/YWCA; join club
    or group 169
(2) Talk to family and friends
    for advice 51
(3) Try different things and see
    which you like best 163
(4) Go to hobby shop for ideas . .164
(5) Look in the Yellow Pages of
    the phone book 165
(6) See if city or county
    provides services 37

243. RELIGIOUS BELIEFS--CONFUSED
     BY BELIEFS

Alternative solutions:

(1) Talk to minister, priest, or
    rabbi for help 89

(2) Talk to a professional
counselor 13
(3) Talk to family and friends
for advice 51
(4) Go to public library for
information 12

244. SELF-CONFIDENCE--LACKING

Alternative solutions:

(1) Change the situation 162
(2) Talk to family and friends
for advice 51
(3) Try different things and see
which you like best 163
(4) Become a volunteer in a
community service agency . . .175
(5) Talk to a professional
counselor 13
(6) Talk to minister, priest, or
rabbi for help 89

245. SHY--FEELS TOO SHY

See: "SELF-IMPROVEMENT PROBLEMS"

Self-confidence--Lacking

246. SOCIAL LIFE--NOT ENOUGH

Alternative solutions:

(1) Talk to family and friends
for advice 51
(2) Talk to a professional
counselor 13
(3) Make yourself do whatever is
necessary in hopes of solving
your problem that way 161
(4) See if city or county
provides services 37
(5) Join social activities provided by church or school . . .170
(6) Try different things and see
which you like best 163

247. SPEECH TROUBLE

Alternative solutions:

(1) Talk to a physician 82
(2) Find a speech therapist 171
(3) Talk to school psychologist . . 42
(4) Talk to a professional
counselor 13
(5) Talk to Public Health
Department 97
(6) Go to public library for
information 12

248. TEMPER PROBLEMS

Alternative solutions:

(1) Talk to a professional
counselor 13
(2) Talk to minister, priest, or
rabbi for help 89
(3) Talk to family and friends
for advice 51
(4) Change the situation 162
(5) Ignore the problem, wait and
hope 11

249. TIME--NOT USING TIME SATISFACTORILY

See: "SELF-IMPROVEMENT PROBLEMS"

Lazy--Not getting anything done

250. TUTOR--WANTS TO OBTAIN

Alternative solutions:

(1) Talk to the teacher 41
(2) Talk to family and friends
for advice 51
(3) Go to public library for
information 12

251. UNDERWEIGHT

See: "SELF-IMPROVEMENT PROBLEMS"

Overweight

252. UNHAPPY

Alternative solutions:

(1) Talk to a professional
counselor 13
(2) Talk to minister, priest, or
rabbi for help 89
(3) Talk to family and friends
for advice 51
(4) Try different things and see
which you like best 163

253. UNPOPULAR--FEELS UNPOPULAR: WANTS TO BE MORE POPULAR

Alternative solutions:

(1) Talk to a professional
counselor 13
(2) Talk to minister, priest, or
rabbi for help 89
(3) Talk to family and friends
for advice 51

(4) Become a volunteer in a
    community service agency 175
(5) Make yourself do whatever is
    necessary in hopes of solving
    your problem that way 161
(6) Go to public library for
    information 12

254. VIOLENT--GETS VIOLENT
     WHEN MAD

See: "SELF-IMPROVEMENT PROBLEMS"

      Anger Problem--Hard to
      handle anger

17

Section II: The Alternative Solutions and Their Possible Consequences

MASTER LIST OF ITEMS IN SECTION II

Following is a list of the alternative solutions dealt with in this section in the order in which they appear.

1. Arrange child care
2. Hire someone to do the housework
3. Rearrange work hours
4. Change to part-time job
5. Quit job
6. Find a new job
7. Talk to employer about problem
8. Talk to people who are discriminating
9. Obtain legal assistance
10. Transfer job with same employer
11. Ignore the problem, wait and hope
12. Go to public library for information
13. Talk to a professional counselor
14. Find a job, and see if you like the work
15. Talk to working people
16. Ask for on-the-job training
17. Go to school
18. Find different job to gain experience
19. Find different job, and go to school part-time
20. Take different position with desired employer
21. Correct problem at present job
22. Apply from newspaper want ads
23. Contact state employment, school placement and Veterans Administration offices
24. Contact private employment agencies
25. Ask friends for help finding a job
26. Ask previous employers for job
27. Write an unsigned letter to neighbor
28. Arrange to go back on original shift
29. Correct problems at home
30. Ask to change supervisor
31. Find public transportation
32. Buy a car
33. Rent a car
34. Use a cab
35. Use a bicycle
36. Find someone who would drive you
37. See if city or county provides services
38. Call local recruiter
39. Contact small business bureau and banks
40. Ask business owners for suggestions
41. Talk to the teacher
42. Talk to school psychologist
43. Try to teach child better study habits
44. Punish child
45. Reward child for good behavior
46. Find a tutor
47. Talk to a family member about problem
48. Talk to the principal
49. Talk to a guidance counselor
50. Write for catalogues and information
51. Talk to family and friends for advice
52. Be a part-time student
53. Quit school, and take time off
54. Quit school, and find a job
55. Do the best that you can in school
56. Quit school, and take Graduate Equivalency Diploma
57. Don't take subjects you don't like
58. Transfer to a different school
59. Continue to let grades get worse
60. Talk to guidance counselor to change program or about grades
61. Improve your study habits
62. Look in Yellow Pages and newspaper

63. Call the local churches
64. Study in library or other place besides home
65. Arrange with family for time and place to study at home
66. Don't attend classes
67. Change teachers
68. Call Veterans Administration office
69. Try to teach yourself a trade
70. Find day care facility
71. Put child in nursery school
72. Ask friend or relative to care for child
73. Hire a baby sitter
74. Talk to a school nurse
75. Drop out of school
76. Move parent to your home
77. Ask relative to take parent into his or her home
78. Pay someone to live with parent
79. Place parent in a nursing home
80. Hire someone part-time
81. Talk to nursing home directors
82. Talk to a physician
83. Ask parent, spouse, or child to leave the home
84. Contact places
85. Obtain financial public assistance in meantime
86. Contact spouse, and try to solve problem
87. Relocate to attend vocational school
88. Run away from home
89. Talk to minister, priest, or rabbi for help
90. Arrange activities for yourself
91. Live separately from spouse
92. Live with person
93. Attend class to learn parenting skills
94. Talk to state agency for the handicapped
95. Call the police
96. Talk to Planned Parenthood
97. Talk to Public Health Department
98. Report it to Welfare Department
99. Talk to neighbor
100. Set aside time to be together
101. Rearrange finances so you don't have to work so hard
102. Get a divorce
103. You obtain job to ease financial situation
104. Talk to banks to obtain loan
105. Write down budget and keep track of expenses
106. Increase amount of money available
107. Contact League of Women Voters, Red Cross, Salvation Army, Council of Churches
108. Get a loan from friends or relativ
109. Call Veterans Administration for loan or benefits
110. Get a loan from school, scholarshi or community
111. Get a full-time job
112. Get a part-time job
113. Obtain food stamps
114. Be financially dependent upon someone else
115. Check your insurance policy for coverage
116. Talk to the Legal Aid Society for legal advice
117. Call Medicaid, Medicare, Social Security, or Welfare, and complain
118. Ask for a raise on your job
119. Talk to banker or investment counselor
120. Investigate retirement program whe you work
121. Talk to Social Security Administration
122. Talk to an accountant
123. Talk to Internal Revenue Service
124. Take job and risk the Welfare Department's finding out
125. Write to your Congressperson
126. Talk to welfare counselor for information
127. Tell your parents how the situatio is affecting you
128. Talk to pharmacist for suggestions
129. Call Alcoholics Anonymous
130. Check into a hospital for treatmen
131. Go to well-baby clinic
132. Call Obstetrics Department in hospital
133. Talk to rape center counselor
134. Talk to a sex therapist
135. Call Federal Housing Authority
136. Find a new place to live
137. Move in with relatives or friends
138. Talk to landlord
139. Speak to Tenant's Rights Associati
140. Ask friends and relatives for help
141. Put an ad in the newspaper for hel
142. Read ads in newspaper or Yellow Pages
143. Call high school for names of students
144. Read "For Rent" and "For Sale" ads in newspaper
145. Go up and down streets looking for "For Rent" and "For Sale" signs
146. Call landlords and see if they hav anything open
147. Stay in YM/YWCA, motel, or hotel
148. Make repairs, and ask landlord to pay

149. Make repairs, and pay for them yourself
150. Call city Housing Inspector
151. Talk to area real estate agents
152. Buy house from landlord
153. Find a different place to stay temporarily
154. Have home moved
155. Threaten person involved
156. Ask child to move out
157. Call the local Equal Employment Opportunity Office
158. Talk to a cosmetologist
159. Join Weight Watchers
160. Get more exercise
161. Make yourself do whatever is necessary in hopes of solving your problem that way
162. Change the situation
163. Try different things and see which you like best
164. Go to hobby shop for ideas
165. Look in the Yellow Pages of the phone book
166. Complain
167. Make appointment at County Mental Health Clinic
168. Design your own diet or follow a formal diet
169. Join YMCA or YWCA; join club or group
170. Join social activities provided by church or school
171. Find a speech therapist
172. Call area chapter of Alanon
173. Call local crisis hot-line
174. Help child establish new activities and hobbies
175. Become a volunteer in a community service agency
176. Contact creditors to arrange partial payments

SOLUTIONS AND THEIR CONSEQUENCES

1. ARRANGE CHILD CARE

Possible consequences:

(1) You would have someone caring for your child while you are gone.
(2) It may make you feel more secure.
(3) It may cost something.
(4) Child may make new friends.
(5) Child may be unhappy being away from you.

2. HIRE SOMEONE TO DO THE HOUSEWORK

Possible consequences:

(1) You would have help cleaning house.
(2) It would leave you more time.
(3) Your home would be clean.
(4) It may be costly.
(5) You may not want someone else in your home.

3. REARRANGE WORK HOURS

Possible consequences:

(1) It would solve problem.
(2) It may cause other problems.

4. CHANGE TO PART-TIME JOB

Possible consequences:

(1) It may solve problem.

(2) It may cause financial difficulties by reducing the amount of money you will earn.
(3) It would give you added time during working hours.

5. QUIT JOB

Possible consequences:

(1) It would increase your free time.
(2) It would give you more time with family and friends
(3) You would lose job's income; this may cause financial problems.
(4) You may eventually have to find another job.
(5) You may have to explain to people why you are not working.
(6) You may have nothing to do with your free time.
(7) It may ruin your chance for a good reference from your employer.
(8) It may leave you feeling dissatisfied with yourself.

6. FIND A NEW JOB

Possible consequences:

(1) It may end problem.
(2) You may not be able to find another job.

(3) You may not be able to find similar job.
(4) You may lose the benefits of present job.
(5) It may mean being unemployed for a period of time.
(6) You may find a better job that you would prefer.

7. TALK TO EMPLOYER ABOUT PROBLEM

Possible consequences:

(1) It may stop problem.
(2) It may not stop problem.
(3) You may lose your job.
(4) You may be transferred to a different job.
(5) You may receive help finding new job.
(6) You will make your feelings known to your employer, which may make you feel better

8. TALK TO PEOPLE WHO ARE DISCRIMINATING

Possible consequences:

(1) It may end discrimination.
(2) It may cause bad feelings and lead to a worse situation.
(3) It may help you feel that you are doing something about the situation.

9. OBTAIN LEGAL ASSISTANCE

Possible consequences:

(1) Problem would be handled for you.
(2) Illegal practice would have to be changed if court so ordered.
(3) Problem could become public knowledge.
(4) It may be costly.
(5) It could create uncomfortable working or personal situation.

10. TRANSFER JOB WITH SAME EMPLOYER

Possible consequences:

(1) It may solve the problem.
(2) It may not solve the problem.
(3) You may enjoy the new job more.
(4) You may meet new people in the new position.
(5) You may not like the new job better.

11. IGNORE THE PROBLEM, WAIT AND HOPE

Possible consequences:

(1) Problem may stop on its own.
(2) You may get very nervous not doing anything about problem.
(3) Problem may get worse with time.
(4) You may not be able to ignore problem
(5) Problem may eventually not bother you
(6) Continuing problem may affect your mood and thereby cause you additional problems.
(7) You may find that problem was easily handled by ignoring it and just carrying on.

12. GO TO PUBLIC LIBRARY FOR INFORMATION

Possible consequences:

(1) You may find the information you want
(2) You may not find the information you want.
(3) Librarian may be able to tell you where to find the information you want.
(4) You may find information on other topics at the same time as you seek answers to original question.

13. TALK TO A PROFESSIONAL COUNSELOR

Possible consequences:

(1) You would get professional help solving the problem.
(2) Counselor may be able to provide information and help with a number of problems, not just this one.
(3) Counselor may know of other people and resources in area who can help.
(4) It may cost something.
(5) You may be able to have professional counseling on a regular basis for continuing help.
(6) You may not want other people to know you are going to a counselor.
(7) The counselor can help you obtain medication for relief if necessary.
(8) Counselor may not help at all.
(9) Conversation is confidential.

14. FIND A JOB, AND SEE IF YOU LIKE THE WORK

Possible consequences:

(1) It may tell you waht kind of work you like.
(2) It may be a good job.

(3) You would have an income.

(4) You would meet new people.

(5) It may help you decide what you don't like.

(6) It may give you a chance to observe what other people in other jobs do, which may help you think about whether you'd like that work.

(7) It may help you know whether you'll need advanced training.

(8) It will provide you with some income while you are making up your mind.

15. TALK TO WORKING PEOPLE

Possible consequences:

(1) It would give you information about job.

(2) It may tell you things about jobs that books don't.

(3) It may give you mistaken idea about job.

(4) It may give you information about other jobs, also.

(5) It may answer your questions.

16. ASK FOR ON-THE-JOB TRAINING

Possible consequences:

(1) You would gain desired work experience.

(2) You would be working for desired employer.

(3) You would be making money while gaining skills.

(4) You would not have to attend school.

(5) You may collect fringe benefits of job (sick pay, insurance, etc.) while gaining experience.

(6) Company may be able to collect money from government to train you.

(7) It would show employer you are very interested in desired job.

(8) You might learn you are not ready for that particular job.

17. GO TO SCHOOL

Possible consequences:

(1) You would gain necessary background for desired job.

(2) Added schooling may increase your wages.

(3) It may open way to a new and better job.

(4) You still may not have the necessary work experience for desired job.

(5) It may cost something.

(6) It takes time.

18. FIND DIFFERENT JOB TO GAIN EXPERIENCE

Possible consequences:

(1) You would gain desired experience.

(2) You may find a job you like better.

(3) You would have income while gaining experience.

(4) You may still not have necessary experience for desired job.

(5) It would show employer you are really interested in desired job.

19. FIND DIFFERENT JOB, AND GO TO SCHOOL PART-TIME

Possible consequences:

(1) You may find a job you like better.

(2) You would have an income while going to school.

(3) You would gain necessary education for desired job.

(4) It would show desired employer you are really interested in desired job.

(5) School may increase the wages you can earn.

(6) It may cost something to go to school.

(7) It may be very difficult to schedule job and school at the same time.

20. TAKE DIFFERENT POSITION WITH DESIRED EMPLOYER

Possible consequences:

(1) You would be working for the desired employer.

(2) You may be able to arrange on-the-job training for desired position.

(3) You may be promoted to desired position.

(4) You could accumulate vacation time, sick days, etc., with desired employer.

(5) You may not be able to transfer to desired job.
(6) You would show employer you are interested in company.
(7) You would have work experience for the next time you look for a job.

21. CORRECT PROBLEM AT PRESENT JOB

Possible consequences:

(1) It would save your job.
(2) You would not have to look for a new job.
(3) You would save the benefits (vacation, sick time, etc.) accumulated on present job.
(4) You may have to put up with negative feelings toward the present job and employees.
(5) You may have to put up with negative reputation at work.
(6) You may have to change something you do not want to change to keep your job and correct the problem.

22. APPLY FROM NEWSPAPER WANT ADS

Possible consequences:

(1) You may find a good job.
(2) You may find job you never would have thought of applying for.
(3) It costs nothing to apply.
(4) It will help you feel like you are doing something about finding a job.
(5) You may find a company with an immediate opening.

23. CONTACT STATE EMPLOYMENT, SCHOOL PLACEMENT, AND VETERANS ADMINISTRATION OFFICES

Possible consequences:

(1) They may have a job starting immediately.
(2) You may find a good job you never would have thought of.
(3) It costs nothing.
(4) Your name will be with office for any job that they hear about in the future.
(5) It will make you feel that you are doing something about finding a job.
(6) It lets more people look for a job for you, which may mean you will find a job sooner.

(7) They may have free counseling available to assist you with your job-finding problems.
(8) If they can't find you a job, you may feel even more discouraged.

24. CONTACT PRIVATE EMPLOYMENT AGENCIES

Possible consequences:

(1) They may have a job starting immediately.
(2) Your name and qualifications would be on record with them for future job openings.
(3) More people would be looking for a job for you.
(4) It will help you feel that you are doing something to find a job.
(5) It may be costly.
(6) They may not be able to help you find a job.
(7) You may have to spend valuable time waiting for them to find a job opening for you.
(8) If they can't find you a job, you may feel even more discouraged.

25. ASK FRIENDS FOR HELP FINDING A JOB

Possible consequences:

(1) More people helping you find a job may mean you find a job sooner.
(2) Friends may know of unadvertised job openings.
(3) Friends might ask their employers to hire you, which could result in a job for you.
(4) Friends may be able to hire you themselves.
(5) You may feel embarrassed to ask friends for help.

26. ASK PREVIOUS EMPLOYERS FOR JOB

Possible consequences:

(1) You may get rehired.
(2) They may know of job openings for which you could apply.
(3) More people will be helping you find a job, which may mean you'll find one sooner.
(4) You may feel embarrassed to ask previous employers for help.

27. WRITE AN UNSIGNED LETTER TO NEIGHBOR

Possible consequences:

(1) It would let your neighbor know that you are aware of their problem.
(2) It may lead neighbor to stop problem behavior.
(3) It would prevent the neighbor from knowing the letter was from you.
(4) You may feel uncomfortable sending an unsigned letter.

28. ARRANGE TO GO BACK ON ORIGINAL SHIFT

Possible consequences:

(1) It may solve problems caused by shift change.
(2) It may cause bad feelings from other employees who had their shift changed.
(3) It may cause bad feelings from employer.

29. CORRECT PROBLEMS AT HOME

Possible consequences:

(1) It would allow you to work the new shift.
(2) You would not have to ask employer to change your shift.
(3) It would give you peace of mind that things at home are okay while you are working.

30. ASK TO CHANGE SUPERVISOR

Possible consequences:

(1) It may solve work problem.
(2) It may make work more pleasant for you.
(3) It may cause bad feelings between you and your supervisor.
(4) It may allow you to do different things on the job than you could before.

31. FIND PUBLIC TRANSPORTATION

Possible consequences:

(1) It will get you where you need to go.
(2) Cost may be low.
(3) It does not always to everywhere you might want to go.

(4) It may not be door-to-door transportation.
(5) Time schedule of public transportation may not match yours, so you may arrive early or late.

32. BUY A CAR

Possible consequences:

(1) You will have your own transportation.
(2) You can go where you want to when you want to.
(3) You will have door-to-door transportation.
(4) A car is costly to buy and maintain; you may have to make financial adjustments and sacrifices.
(5) You will have to get car insured, which is an additional cost.

33. RENT A CAR

Possible consequences:

(1) You will have your own transportation.
(2) You will be able to go where you want to when you want to.
(3) You will have door-to-door transportation.
(4) You won't have to insure car; insurance will be paid for by rental agency.
(5) It may be costly.
(6) You may be able to buy the car while paying rental fees.

34. USE A CAB

Possible consequences:

(1) You can get to where you want to go.
(2) It is door-to-door transportation.
(3) You have to depend on someone else to get you where you want to go.
(4) It may be costly.
(5) You would not have costs or inconvenience of owning a car.

35. USE A BICYCLE

Possible consequences:

(1) You may be able to get where you want to go.
(2) It provides exercise.

(3) It is door-to-door transportation.
(4) It is low cost.
(5) It may not be possible to use bicycle in all weather, so you may need alternative means of transportation on some days.

36. FIND SOMEONE WHO WOULD DRIVE YOU

Possible consequences:

(1) It would get you where you want to go.
(2) It would make you dependent upon someone else.
(3) You may feel like a burden on your driver.
(4) It may save gasoline and be economical.
(5) It may not be available just when you want.

37. SEE IF CITY OR COUNTY PROVIDES SERVICES

Possible consequences:

(1) They may provide service you need.
(2) Services may be for only certain citizens (elderly, disabled, poor, etc.)
(3) They may be able to put you in touch with another office that can help.
(4) You may not want city or county officials to know about your problem.
(5) It may be low cost or free.

38. CALL LOCAL RECRUITER

Possible consequences:

(1) You would find information about military service, careers, and benefits.
(2) They could help you decide about joining military.
(3) They will provide information about service-related services and programs (like special training or health benefits).

39. CONTACT SMALL BUSINESS BUREAU AND BANKS

Possible consequences:

(1) They would provide you with necessary information.

(2) They could provide required application forms.
(3) They could answer many of your questions.
(4) They could help you determine your eligibility.
(5) They could put you in touch with other helping organizations.

40. ASK BUSINESS OWNERS FOR SUGGESTIONS

Possible consequences:

(1) They may give you information and suggestions you may not receive elsewhere.
(2) You may meet interesting new people.
(3) You may feel uncomfortable talking to business owners you have not met before.
(4) You may present a threat to business owners if they see you as competition.

41. TALK TO THE TEACHER

Possible consequences:

(1) Teacher may have good suggestions as to how to correct the problem.
(2) Teacher may be willing to work with you to solve the problem.
(3) Teacher may know of other people and resources in the area who can help.
(4) You may develop a good relationship with the teacher.
(5) It may help you feel like you are doing something about the problem.
(6) Teacher may act differently toward child after you talk.
(7) Child may be angry that you talked to the teacher about the problem.
(8) Child may feel you really care when he or she sees you take the trouble to visit with the teacher.

42. TALK TO SCHOOL PSYCHOLOGIST

Possible consequences:

(1) You would get professional help solving problem.
(2) It would be free.
(3) Psychologist may know of other people and resources to help you.

(4) You may be able to have professional help on a regular basis.
(5) You would have someone in school
to talk to about school problems.
(6) You may not want people to know
you are going to see the school
psychologist.
(7) All conversation is confidential.
(8) Psychologist would be able to do
testing to answer any questions
about learning problems.
(9) It might result in special treatment of your child; this may or
may not be desirable.

43. TRY TO TEACH CHILD BETTER STUDY HABITS

Possible consequences:

(1) You will feel like you are helping your child.
(2) You may solve the problem.
(3) You may form a nice relationship
with child.
(4) It may be a rewarding experience
for you.
(5) It would require time and patience.
(6) It may not be helpful to child.
(7) Child may feel you are interfering.
(8) Child may feel reassured by your
interest.
(9) Teacher may feel you are interfering.

44. PUNISH CHILD

Possible consequences:

(1) It may solve the problem.
(2) You may feel like you are doing
something to solve the problem.
(3) It may cause negative feelings
toward you from your child.
(4) Problem may return again in near
future.
(5) You may end up feeling badly about
yourself.

45. REWARD CHILD FOR GOOD BEHAVIOR

Possible consequences:

(1) It teaches your child good
behavior.
(2) Child will enjoy doing good
behavior because your child knows
it is recognized.

(3) Child may have positive feelings
toward you.
(4) You may enjoy making your child
happy.
(5) You may feel like you are bribing
your child to do certain things.

46. FIND A TUTOR

Possible consequences:

(1) It may solve the problem.
(2) Someone else would be solving
the problem for you.
(3) It may cost something.
(4) It may not solve the problem.
(5) It may help you feel like you
are doing something about the
problem.

47. TALK TO FAMILY MEMBER ABOUT PROBLEM

Possible consequences:

(1) You and the other person may gain
better understanding of problem.
(2) It may show family member you are
interested and concerned.
(3) You may find a solution to the
problem.
(4) You may develop a good relationship with the family member.
(5) It may make family member mad
at you.
(6) You may be able to reach a compromise so everyone will be
satisfied.

48. TALK TO THE PRINCIPAL

Possible consequences:

(1) Principal may have good suggestions as to how to correct the
problem.
(2) Principal may have power and
authority to change situation.
(3) Principal may be willing to work
with you to solve the problem.
(4) You may develop a good relationship with the principal.
(5) It may make you feel like you are
doing something about the problem.
(6) Principal may know other people
and resources who can be of help
to you.

(7) Child may be angry at you that you talked to the principal about the problem.
(8) Child may appreciate your efforts.

49. TALK TO A GUIDANCE COUNSELOR

Possible consequences:

(1) You would get professional help.
(2) It is free.
(3) Guidance counselor may be able to provide the information you need.
(4) Counselor may be able to tell you where and how to get the information or advice you need.
(5) Counselor may know other people and resources to help you.
(6) Counselor will know of academic programs that might help you.
(7) Counselor might suggest solutions that you find unacceptable.

50. WRITE FOR CATALOGUES AND INFORMATION

Possible consequences:

(1) You would get desired information.
(2) You would own the information; you would not have to return it by a certain date.
(3) You would let training institutes know of your interest in their program.
(4) It takes time.
(5) You have to have paper, envelopes, and stamps.

51. TALK TO FAMILY AND FRIENDS FOR ADVICE

Possible solutions:

(1) Someone may have had similar experience and could tell you how to handle the situation.
(2) They may provide needed information.
(3) They may talk to their friends, which means additional information would be available to you.
(4) They may feel good that you asked them for help.
(5) More information from people with different experiences may help you make the best decision or may confuse you further.
(6) You may feel better after talking to someone about the problem.

(7) Someone may know of other people or resources that could be of help to you.
(8) You may not want people close to you to know about your problem.

52. BE A PART-TIME STUDENT

Possible consequences:

(1) You would see if you like being in school.
(2) You may be able to work to have income while in school.
(3) You may be able to keep course load light.
(4) It is less expensive than being a full-time student.
(5) It takes longer to complete program than going to school as full-time student.
(6) You could change later to a full-time program if you wanted.

53. QUIT SCHOOL, AND TAKE TIME OFF

Possible consequences:

(1) You will not have to attend school.
(2) You will have free time to do what you want.
(3) You may have limited funds.
(4) You may be bored and have nothing to do.
(5) You may have no one to spend time with.
(6) It may cause a bad reputation.

54. QUIT SCHOOL, AND FIND A JOB

Possible consequences:

(1) You will not have to attend school.
(2) You might find a good job.
(3) You would have income and benefits from the job.
(4) You may meet new people on the job.
(5) You may lose touch with school friends.
(6) It may give you a chance to determine what you want to do.
(7) You will not have an academic degree.
(8) It may cause a bad reputation in school.
(9) It may limit you to low-level jobs.

55. DO THE BEST THAT YOU CAN IN SCHOOL

Possible consequences:

(1) You will get credit for having taken course.
(2) It will mean you have taken subject, which may be important to future goals.
(3) It will show teacher you are serious and trying.
(4) It will mean you will have to continue in the disliked subject.
(5) It is a step toward graduating.

56. QUIT SCHOOL, AND TAKE GRADUATE EQUIVALENCY DIPLOMA

Possible consequences:

(1) You will not have to attend school.
(2) You can get a job and make money.
(3) Graduate Equivalency Diploma will mean you have a high school degree.
(4) Graduate Equivalency Diploma may increase your wages.
(5) You may feel proud of your accomplishment.

57. DON'T TAKE SUBJECTS YOU DON'T LIKE

Possible consequences:

(1) You won't have to be in subjects you don't like.
(2) It may make school more enjoyable.
(3) It may mean you will be missing a required course needed to graduate.
(4) It may mean you will be missing subjects that are required to take advanced courses you would like to take later.
(5) It may mean you will be missing subjects that are important to future goals.
(6) You might end up feeling dissatisfied with yourself for backing out.

58. TRANSFER TO A DIFFERENT SCHOOL

Possible consequences:

(1) You may not have same problems as at first school.
(2) You may meet new people.
(3) You may find yourself in a more pleasant school situation.
(4) You may lose touch with other friends.

(5) You can complete your academic career.
(6) You may have to commute to new school.
(7) You may be able to take different courses than at first school.
(8) You may lose some credit hours when transfer is made.

59. CONTINUE TO LET GRADES GET WORSE

Possible consequences:

(1) You may fail courses.
(2) It may make you feel nervous.
(3) Parents and teachers may put pressure on you.
(4) Failing grades may interfere with future goals.

60. TALK TO GUIDANCE COUNSELOR TO CHANGE PROGRAM OR ABOUT GRADES

Possible consequences:

(1) Counselor will have information about school policies on subjects and grades.
(2) Counselor may be able to rearrange your subject requirements.
(3) Counselor will be able to determine if subject problem will interfere with future plans.
(4) Counselor will be able to help you add or drop a course if necessary.
(5) Counselor may be able to help you solve other problems as well.
(6) Counselor will know of any available programs to help students study better, take tests, etc.
(7) You will feel that you are trying to do something about the problem.
(8) It may turn out to be of no help at all.

61. IMPROVE YOUR STUDY HABITS

Possible consequences:

(1) You may improve your grades.
(2) It may make studying more enjoyable.
(3) It may make test taking easier.
(4) You will learn new study habits you can use from now on.
(5) It may make you feel that you are trying to solve your problem.

62. LOOK IN YELLOW PAGES AND NEWSPAPER

Possible consequences:

(1) It will let you know of available resources.
(2) It costs nothing.
(3) You may find no listing and find that you have wasted your time.

63. CALL THE LOCAL CHURCHES

Possible consequences:

(1) They may know resources or people in area who can help you with your problem.
(2) You may find out no helpful information.
(3) You may receive direct assistance from church.
(4) You may not want the churches to know about your problem.

64. STUDY IN LIBRARY OR OTHER PLACE BESIDES HOME

Possible consequences:

(1) You would get studying done.
(2) You would have quiet, undistracting place to study.
(3) It would not be available 24 hours a day.
(4) You would have to arrange transportation to place of study.

65. ARRANGE WITH FAMILY FOR TIME AND PLACE TO STUDY AT HOME

Possible consequences:

(1) You would get your studying done.
(2) You may be able to study at a time convenient to you.
(3) It may cause crowding or inconvenience to rest of the family.
(4) It may be noisy and distracting at home, making it hard to study.

66. DON'T ATTEND CLASSES

Possible consequences:

(1) You may be able to pass course without having to attend classes you dislike.
(2) You may be failed in the class.
(3) You may have to repeat subject you dislike.

(4) Note about attendance may be sent home.
(5) It may lead to negative reputation with some teachers and students in school.

67. CHANGE TEACHERS

Possible consequences:

(1) It may solve problem.
(2) It may cause bad feelings between you and the teacher.
(3) Child may be helped by being in a new situation.
(4) Child may be put behind in classwork in new class.
(5) Child may have fewer friends in new class.

68. CALL VETERANS ADMINISTRATION OFFICE

Possible consequences:

(1) You would find out desired information.
(2) You may be able to meet with a professional person, free of charge, to discuss your questions.
(3) They may know of other helping resources in your area.

69. TRY TO TEACH YOURSELF A TRADE

Possible consequences:

(1) You may be able to do trade without having to go to school.
(2) You may get desired job.
(3) You may impress your employer.
(4) You may feel very proud of yourself.
(5) You may not be able to do it.
(6) You may end up with new hobby you enjoy.
(7) You may still require school certificate to obtain desired job.
(8) While teaching yourself, you may find that it isn't what you really wanted to do.

70. FIND DAY CARE FACILITY

Possible consequences:

(1) Child would be cared for while you are away.
(2) It may help you feel your child is safe.

(3) You may have to deliver and pick up child at certain times.
(4) It may cost something.
(5) Child would be with other children while you are away.
(6) Child may learn many valuable new skills.
(7) Child may learn some undesirable new habits.

71. PUT CHILD IN NURSERY SCHOOL

Possible consequences:

(1) Child would be cared for while you are away.
(2) You may feel child is safe while you are gone.
(3) You may have to deliver and pick up child at certain times.
(4) It may cost something.
(5) Child would be with other children during the time you are away.
(6) Child would be with qualified teacher.
(7) Child may learn many valuable new skills.
(8) Child may learn some undesirable habits.

72. ASK FRIEND OR RELATIVE TO CARE FOR CHILD

Possible consequences:

(1) Child would be cared for while you are gone.
(2) It may not cost anything.
(3) You may feel child is safe while you are away.
(4) You may feel that you are a burden to a friend.
(5) Person caring for your child may get tired of the imposition.
(6) Person may not be able to care for child every day, which means sometimes you will have to arrange alternative child care.
(7) You may feel good knowing who will be taking care of child.
(8) Child may be glad to know the person he or she will be staying with.

73. HIRE A BABY SITTER

Possible consequences:

(1) Child would be cared for while you are away.

(2) It would cost something.
(3) Child care could be arranged for the times most convenient to you.
(4) Perhaps child and babysitter can remain in your home.
(5) It may make you feel child is safe while you're gone.
(6) Baby sitter may not be trained, so care may not be the quality you would prefer.

74. TALK TO A SCHOOL NURSE

Possible consequences:

(1) Nurse may be in a position to help you settle problems at school.
(2) Nurse may be willing to work with you to solve problem.
(3) You may develop good relationship with the nurse.
(4) Nurse may arrange for other people in school to help you.
(5) Nurse may not be able to help.
(6) You may not like the help that the nurse suggests.

75. DROP OUT OF SCHOOL

Possible consequences:

(1) It may end problem at school.
(2) You will not get your academic degree.
(3) It may give you more time.
(4) You might have nothing to do with your free time.
(5) It may give you a bad reputation.
(6) It may make you feel disappointed with yourself.

76. MOVE PARENT TO YOUR HOME

Possible consequences:

(1) It would solve problem of needing someone to care for your parent.
(2) It may cause problems in your home with your spouse and family.
(3) It may be an added expense.
(4) You may feel unable to provide the care needed by your parent.
(5) Conditions in your home may not be the best for your parent.

77. ASK RELATIVE TO TAKE PARENT INTO HIS OR HER HOME

Possible consequences:

(1) Someone would be caring for parent.
(2) It may cause problems in relative's home.
(3) You may feel uncomfortable asking relative to take parent into home.
(4) You could assist with care and finances.
(5) Parent may feel you are just trying to get him or her out of your way.

78. PAY SOMEONE TO LIVE WITH PARENT

Possible consequences:

(1) It would provide care for parent.
(2) It would cost something.
(3) You would have to entrust care of parent to someone you may not know very well.
(4) Twenty-four hour care could be provided.
(5) Parent could continue living in his or her own home.
(6) Parent would have company.

79. PLACE PARENT IN A NURSING HOME

Possible consequences:

(1) Parent would be cared for on full-time basis by staff trained to serve the elderly.
(2) It may be costly.
(3) Cost might be covered by Medicare or Medicaid.
(4) Parent would have to give up his or her home.
(5) You may have bad feelings about putting your parent in a nursing home.

80. HIRE SOMEONE PART-TIME

Possible consequences:

(1) It may provide adequate care for parent.
(2) You may have to find care or do it yourself during the time hired person is not working for you.
(3) It may be added expense for you.
(4) It would provide part-time company for parent.
(5) Parent could stay in his or her own home.

81. TALK TO NURSING HOME DIRECTORS

Possible consequences:

(1) You would get professional advice from someone who should know exactly what services are available.
(2) The director may know of other people and resources in the area to help you.
(3) The additional information may make your decisions easier.

82. TALK TO A PHYSICIAN

Possible consequences:

(1) You would get professional opinion about your problem.
(2) Physician may be able to provide needed information.
(3) Physician may be able to help you with a number of problems.
(4) Physician may know of other people and resources in your area who could help you.
(5) It may cost something, but the cost may be covered by Medicare, Medicaid, or insurance.
(6) Physician can prescribe medication for relief of problem if necessary.
(7) It may help you feel like you are doing something about the problem.
(8) Visit could be kept confidential.

83. ASK PARENT, SPOUSE, OR CHILD TO LEAVE THE HOME

Possible consequences:

(1) It may solve problem at home.
(2) It may cause bad relationship between you and that person.
(3) It may cause losing touch with child or parent.
(4) You wouldn't have to see child or parent when they are doing the behaviors you disapprove of.

84. CONTACT PLACES

Possible consequences:

(1) They may have heard from your child.
(2) They may ask around for you so that more people will be looking for your child.

(3) It will help you feel like you are doing something to locate your child.

(4) You may feel embarrassed to tell people that your child has run away from home.

85. OBTAIN FINANCIAL PUBLIC ASSISTANCE IN MEANTIME

Possible consequences:

(1) It would help with immediate financial needs.

(2) You may not want to let others know of your financial situation, and obtaining public assistance might make it public knowledge.

(3) You would have to disclose your financial assets to whomever you apply for assistance.

(4) It may make you lose pride in yourself.

(5) The agency may put you in touch with other helpful programs that you didn't know about before.

(6) The public assistance reporting process may cause you to lose some household privacy.

86. CONTACT SPOUSE, AND TRY TO SOLVE PROBLEM

Possible consequences:

(1) It may solve the problem.

(2) It could create new problems between you and your spouse.

(3) Contact with spouse could make your dealings with each other more pleasant.

87. RELOCATE TO ATTEND VOCATIONAL SCHOOL

Possible consequences:

(1) You would be able to go to school where you want.

(2) You will have to move and leave present home and friends.

(3) Relocating usually costs something.

(4) In the new area, you will have opportunity to meet new friends and do new things.

88. RUN AWAY FROM HOME

Possible consequences:

(1) You will no longer live at home.

(2) You may not be able to find a place to live or a way to eat and clothe yourself.

(3) You may have financial problems living on your own.

(4) It may cause problems at home because you are not there.

(5) It may solve your problem.

89. TALK TO MINISTER, PRIEST, OR RABBI FOR HELP

Possible consequences:

(1) You may get help with your situation and feelings.

(2) He or she may be able to provide help and information with a number of problems, not just this one.

(3) He or she would know of other people and resources in the area who could be of help.

(4) It may help you feel that you are doing something about the situation.

(5) It will not cost anything.

(6) You may be able to talk to him or her on a regular basis.

(7) You may feel you do not know any clergymen or clergywomen well enough to ask to talk to them.

90. ARRANGE ACTIVITIES FOR YOURSELF

Possible consequences:

(1) Your spouse's absence may bother you less.

(2) You may develop new interests and friends.

(3) You may have to explain to people why you are involving yourself in new activities.

(4) Someone in your family may not want you arranging activities for yourself.

(5) You may find a whole new lease on life when you establish new friends and activities.

(6) You may find that worry, depression, and loneliness abate once you have found new friends and activities.

91. LIVE SEPARATELY FROM SPOUSE

Possible consequences:

(1) It will let you see how living without a spouse may be.

(2) It may help you decide about getting a divorce.
(3) Spouse may not want to live separately, and may cause other problems.
(4) It may solve problem.
(5) It may help you see spouse in different light.

92. LIVE WITH PERSON

Possible consequences:

(1) You will see what living with the person may be like; it might help you decide about marriage.
(2) You may not think it is a morally good thing to do.
(3) Other people may not approve of your living with this person.
(4) It might not help you decide about getting married.

93. ATTEND CLASS TO LEARN PARENTING SKILLS

Possible consequences:

(1) It will teach you successful ways of raising and disciplining children.
(2) It may cost something.
(3) It will take time.
(4) It may provide individual instruction so you'd get help with your specific problems.
(5) It may put you in touch with other parents who have experienced similar problems so you'll have understanding people to talk with.

94. TALK TO STATE AGENCY FOR THE HANDICAPPED

Possible consequences:

(1) Counselor will know of agencies and individuals in your area who can help you with your problem.
(2) Counselor can provide information to answer questions.
(3) Agency may have funding available for any special services or needs you may have.

95. CALL THE POLICE

Possible consequences:

(1) Police may be able to provide help in your situation.

(2) Calling the police may anger person causing the problem, which might lead to a new problem.
(3) Neighbors might know police have come.
(4) The police might not take you seriously.

96. TALK TO PLANNED PARENTHOOD

Possible consequences:

(1) They will have physician and nurses to whom you can talk.
(2) They will have reliable information about abortion, birth control, and childbirth.
(3) You may have to have an appointment to talk to someone.
(4) It is confidential.
(5) It may cost something.
(6) They give pregnancy tests.
(7) They can provide all forms of birth control.

97. TALK TO PUBLIC HEALTH DEPARTMENT

Possible consequences:

(1) Doctors and nurses are available for information and examinations.
(2) You may receive a prescription for relief of the problem.
(3) It is free.
(4) You may not be eligible for certain services if you earn more than their income limit.
(5) They can help you check into a hospital, if it is needed.
(6) They can help you locate a specialist, if one is needed.
(7) It may help you feel that you are doing something about the problem.

98. REPORT IT TO WELFARE DEPARTMENT

Possible consequences:

(1) It may prevent further child abuse.
(2) It may result in child being removed from home.
(3) You can request that the Welfare Department not tell neighbor who it was that contacted them.
(4) It may result in the problem being referred to the courts.
(5) You may feel badly about reporting your neighbor to the authorities.
(6) It may result in an investigation by a social worker.

99. TALK TO NEIGHBOR

Possible consequences:

(1) It may help neighbor by giving him or her someone to talk to about the problem.
(2) You may develop a good relationship with the neighbor.
(3) You may find a solution.
(4) Neighbor may be angry at you for interfering.

100. SET ASIDE TIME TO BE TOGETHER

Possible consequences:

(1) You would have guaranteed times to be together.
(2) It may increase your enjoyment of each other's company.
(3) It may help you both feel better about the amount of time spent together.
(4) It may help you become better friends.
(5) It may give you enough time together to work out your problems.
(6) It may help each of you understand the other better.
(7) The other person may be reassured by seeing that you will set aside special time just for him or her.
(8) It may make other family members jealous.

101. REARRANGE FINANCES SO YOU DON'T HAVE TO WORK SO HARD

Possible consequences:

(1) It may mean that you will have more time to spend together.
(2) You may enjoy each other's company better.
(3) You may personally feel better about changing to a simpler, less expensive way of living.
(4) It may mean you will have to change certain things in your life-style in order to rearrange finances.
(5) With less financial pressure, family members who are employed may enjoy their jobs more.

102. GET A DIVORCE

Possible consequences:

(1) It may solve your marital problems.

(2) It may result in financial problems after divorce.
(3) It can be either good or bad for children.
(4) It may allow you to lead a happier life after the divorce.
(5) You may feel family and friends will disapprove.

103. YOU OBTAIN JOB TO EASE FINANCIAL SITUATION

Possible consequences:

(1) It may ease financial situation so that the family member doesn't have to work so hard.
(2) It may mean spouse has more time to spend with you.
(3) Family members may not want you working.
(4) It may make new problems for you (baby sitter, uniforms, transportation, etc.)

104. TALK TO BANKS TO OBTAIN LOAN

Possible consequences:

(1) You may get loan for the amount of money needed.
(2) You will have to pay interest on money loaned.
(3) You will have to have collateral to get loan.
(4) You may be refused by bank and end up still needing money.
(5) It will increase your debts.
(6) Bankers talk to you for free.
(7) Bankers are knowledgeable about how to get loans and other money matters.

105. WRITE DOWN BUDGET AND KEEP TRACK OF EXPENSES

Possible consequences:

(1) It would allow you to see how you spend your money.
(2) It would help you spend only what you've stated you want to spend on certain items.
(3) Someone else could check it, which might help you stay within your budget.
(4) You may not like what you learn about your own spending habits.
(5) You may have difficulty explaining your budget efforts to other family members.

106. INCREASE AMOUNT OF MONEY AVAILABLE

Possible consequences:

(1) It would ease financial situation.
(2) It may take up desired free time.
(3) It may cause child care problems.
(4) It may allow you to remain financially independent.
(5) If you are on welfare, it may reduce the amount of assistance.

107. CONTACT LEAGUE OF WOMEN VOTERS, RED CROSS, SALVATION ARMY, COUNCIL OF CHURCHES

Possible consequences:

(1) All organizations can help you locate money and supplies for emergency needs.
(2) They may provide you with unexpected additional information about where to get help in your community.

108. GET A LOAN FROM FRIENDS OR RELATIVES

Possible consequences:

(1) It will solve immediate financial needs.
(2) You may not have to pay interest on loan.
(3) You may feel uncomfortable borrowing from someone else.
(4) It will make you somewhat financially dependent on someone else.
(5) It may put an unpleasant strain on your relationship.

109. CALL VETERANS ADMINISTRATION FOR LOAN OR BENEFITS

Possible consequences:

(1) It may solve immediate financial problems.
(2) You may not be eligible and end up still needing money.
(3) Veterans Administration may be able to help you find a job or training.
(4) They may know other financial resources available to you to help with your situation.

110. GET A LOAN FROM SCHOOL, SCHOLARSHIP, OR COMMUNITY

Possible consequences:

(1) It would provide you with at least part of the money you would need to continue education.
(2) It may have low interest or it may not be necessary to pay the scholarship back.
(3) It may mean that you would not have to work while in school.
(4) It may mean having to keep grades up to a certain level.

111. GET A FULL-TIME JOB

Possible consequences:

(1) It would make you financially independent.
(2) It may make you feel pride in yourself.
(3) It may mean having to change your schedule to arrange work hours.
(4) It will mean you'll have less free time.

112. GET A PART-TIME JOB

Possible consequences:

(1) It would make you financially independent.
(2) It may make you feel pride in yourself.
(3) It may be easier to arrange your schedule to accommodate a part-time job rather than a full-time job.

113. OBTAIN FOOD STAMPS

Possible consequences:

(1) It would help you afford your food bills.
(2) It may ease other financial demands, too.
(3) You may not want others to know of your financial situation, and using food stamps would make it public information.
(4) It may make you lose pride in yourself.

114. BE FINANCIALLY DEPENDENT
     UPON SOMEONE ELSE

Possible consequences:

(1) You may have to do what someone
    else tells you.
(2) You will not have your own money.
(3) It may make you feel badly about
    yourself.
(4) It means you don't have to work
    on a steady basis.
(5) Other party may come to feel you
    are a burden.

115. CHECK YOUR INSURANCE POLICY
     FOR COVERAGE

Possible consequences:

(1) It may help ease financial prob-
    lems by paying some bills for you.
(2) You may find that insurance
    company will not help pay any-
    thing, so you are left in same
    financial situation.
(3) You may be able to borrow on your
    insurance.
(4) If they pay certain bills for you,
    your insurance rates may go up.

116. TALK TO THE LEGAL AID SOCIETY
     FOR LEGAL ADVICE

Possible consequences:

(1) Legal problem would be handled
    for you for free.
(2) You may not be eligible for Legal
    Aid and may have to find another
    way to pay for legal advice.
(3) They may be able to help you find
    the kind of private attorney that
    you need.

117. CALL MEDICAID, MEDICARE, SOCIAL
     SECURITY, OR WELFARE, AND COMPLAIN

Possible consequences:

(1) It may solve problem.
(2) It may not solve problem, but may
    help you feel that you are doing
    something about the situation.
(3) It may make the social worker
    angry at you.

118. ASK FOR A RAISE ON YOUR JOB

Possible consequences:

(1) Raise would give you more money
    and may solve your money problems.
(2) You may feel uncomfortable asking
    employer for a raise.
(3) You may receive a raise that you
    deserve but that employer hadn't
    offered you.
(4) It may cause negative feelings
    between you and some of the other
    people at work.

119. TALK TO BANKER OR
     INVESTMENT COUNSELOR

Possible consequences:

(1) They are specifically trained to
    help people manage their money,
    obtain loans, and plan for their
    financial future.
(2) They will talk to you for free.
(3) They should be able to provide
    you with needed advice and
    suggestions.

120. INVESTIGATE RETIREMENT
     PROGRAM WHERE YOU WORK

Possible consequences:

(1) It will help you feel that you
    are doing something.
(2) It may give you more realistic
    information about your financial
    security in old age.

121. TALK TO SOCIAL SECURITY
     ADMINISTRATION

Possible consequences:

(1) They should be able to provide
    an estimate of the benefits for
    which you are eligible.
(2) It may help you feel that you are
    doing something about your problem.

122. TALK TO AN ACCOUNTANT

Possible consequences:

(1) Accountant is trained to handle
    tax problems and should be able
    to help you with your tax problems.
(2) It may cost you something.

123. TALK TO INTERNAL REVENUE SERVICE

Possible consequences:

(1) IRS agents are trained to handle tax problems and should be able to help you with your tax problems.
(2) It may be a free service.
(3) There may not be an IRS office in the area, so you may have to get help over the phone. They have a toll-free phone number in your area.

124. TAKE JOB AND RISK THE WELFARE DEPARTMENT'S FINDING OUT

Possible consequences:

(1) It would increase money, and may make meeting financial needs easier.
(2) If you are caught by the Welfare Department, you could be prosecuted for fraud.
(3) It may make you feel that you are being dishonest.

125. WRITE TO YOUR CONGRESSPERSON

Possible consequences:

(1) If congressperson intervenes on your behalf, you may get fast action from the Welfare Department.
(2) You may get the changes in welfare about which you are complaining.
(3) You may get a personal letter back from your congressperson.

126. TALK TO WELFARE COUNSELOR FOR INFORMATION

Possible consequences:

(1) Counselor will give you more information, which should help you make your decision.
(2) You may have to wait to see welfare counselor because usually you cannot make an appointment.

127. TELL YOUR PARENTS HOW THE SITUATION IS AFFECTING YOU

Possible consequences:

(1) Your honesty may startle your parents into listening more closely to what you have to say.

(2) It may help change the bad situation.
(3) It should help them realize how much their situation is affecting and bothering you.
(4) Your parents may not be ready to hear the truth from you.
(5) It may lead to even more problems.

128. TALK TO PHARMACIST FOR SUGGESTIONS

Possible consequences:

(1) Pharmacist may be able to suggest something that doesn't require a prescription to relieve the discomfort.
(2) You may need a doctor's prescription before pharmacist can give you the medicine you would need.
(3) Pharmacist's advice is free.

129. CALL ALCOHOLICS ANONYMOUS

Possible consequences:

(1) Suggestions and advice could be given confidentially.
(2) Someone in A.A. may have had a similar problem and could give you advice.
(3) A.A. member may know other people and resources in the area who may be of help to you.

130. CHECK INTO A HOSPITAL FOR TREATMENT

Possible consequences:

(1) It may solve your medical or emotional problems.
(2) Twenty-four-hour medical care would be available.
(3) It would interrupt job, family life, etc.
(4) It may cost something.
(5) It may alarm other people that you are in a hospital.
(6) You may feel depressed about having to go to the hospital.

131. GO TO WELL-BABY CLINIC

Possible consequences:

(1) It is staffed by physicians and nurses.

(2) They can take care of most pregnancy and children's health problems.
(3) Often, the service is free.
(4) They can direct you to other health programs.

132. CALL OBSTETRICS DEPARTMENT IN HOSPITAL

Possible consequences:

(1) They can provide medical care.
(2) They may be able to make a referral for you to see a physician who can help you.
(3) They may not be able to help you unless you already have a physician.
(4) They can see you in the emergency room of hospital.
(5) Hospital care is expensive.

133. TALK TO RAPE CENTER COUNSELOR

Possible consequences:

(1) You may get help with problem from someone who has been specially trained to work with rape and crisis victims.
(2) Counselor may know of other people and resources in the area who can be of help to you.

134. TALK TO A SEX THERAPIST

Possible consequences:

(1) You may get help with problem from someone who is specially trained to help people with sexual problems.
(2) Therapist may know of other people and resources in the area who may be of help to you.
(3) It may cost something; the cost may be covered by medical insurance.
(4) You may be worried about someone's finding out that you see a sex therapist.

135. CALL FEDERAL HOUSING AUTHORITY

Possible consequences:

(1) They may be able to help you arrange a loan to buy a house.

(2) The interest rate may be lower than on a loan from a bank.
(3) They may not be able to help you.

136. FIND A NEW PLACE TO LIVE

Possible consequences:

(1) It would get you out of a bad living situation.
(2) It is sometimes a hassel finding a new place to live.
(3) Often, moving involves some expenses.
(4) You have to let everyone know you are moving.

137. MOVE IN WITH RELATIVES OR FRIENDS

Possible consequences:

(1) It would get you out of a bad living situation.
(2) You may feel like you are causing an inconvenience to your friends or relatives.
(3) You may be less free to live in your own life-style when in someone else's home.
(4) You may be able to save some money for living expenses while living with family and friends.
(5) Your imposition on them may cause some negative feelings from them toward you.

138. TALK TO LANDLORD

Possible consequences:

(1) Problem between you and landlord could be talked about and a compromise reached.
(2) Landlord may be unwilling to change his mind about the problem.
(3) It may make you feel good to talk to him before talking to other people for help with problem.
(4) It may create bad feelings between you and your landlord.

139. SPEAK TO TENANT'S RIGHTS ASSOCIATION

Possible consequences:

(1) You would get information and advice from an agency specially designed to be familiar with housing laws and tenants' rights.

(2) It may help you feel that you are doing something about the problem.

(3) They may be able to recommend people and/or agencies who can help you solve your housing problems.

(4) When landlord finds out you have talked with tenants group, he may become angry with you.

140. ASK FRIENDS AND RELATIVES FOR HELP

Possible consequences:

(1) If anyone will help, you could do home improvement for less cost than hiring someone else to do it.

(2) No one might know how to do the work, and some mistake could be made while doing it that might cause problems.

(3) You might feel that you will owe the people something if they work on your house.

(4) Friends and relatives might become annoyed with you for making demands on their time.

141. PUT AN AD IN THE NEWSPAPER FOR HELP

Possible consequences:

(1) You may get response from someone who can make your desired home improvements.

(2) You may not know anything about the people who respond to the ad.

(3) Running an ad in the newspaper costs something.

(4) Person responding might do work less expensively than business firm you might hire.

(5) Person responding may not guarantee his or her work and may not be insured in case any damage to your home or themselves occurred.

142. READ ADS IN NEWSPAPER OR YELLOW PAGES

Possible consequences:

(1) You may learn about who can do the kind of work you want done.

(2) Ad will provide their phone number for you to contact them.

(3) You may not know anything about person you locate from the ad.

(4) You may be able to negotiate price of job with the person.

143. CALL HIGH SCHOOL FOR NAMES OF STUDENTS

Possible consequences:

(1) They may know of someone who can do the kind of work you want done.

(2) You may not know anything about the person recommended to you.

(3) Person responding may do work less expensively than a business firm you might hire.

(4) Student may not guarantee his or her work and may not be insured in case any damage to your home or themselves occurred.

(5) You would be hiring someone who really needs the money, or else the student wouldn't have his or her name on the list at school.

144. READ "FOR RENT" OR "FOR SALE" ADS IN NEWSPAPER

Possible consequences:

(1) You may find place to rent or buy.

(2) The place may have already been rented or sold.

(3) You may be able to avoid realtor's fees by finding a place through a newspaper ad.

(4) It is convenient and easy to do.

145. GO UP AND DOWN STREETS LOOKING FOR "FOR RENT" AND "FOR SALE" SIGNS

Possible consequences:

(1) You may find a place to rent or buy.

(2) You may be able to avoid realtor's fees by finding person who is renting or selling their own home.

(3) It takes time to walk around and look.

(4) It could require a means of transportation besides just walking.

(5) If there is a sign in front of the place, it probably means that it is still available.

(6) It may help you locate a place that couldn't be found any other way.

146. CALL LANDLORDS AND SEE IF
      THEY HAVE ANYTHING OPEN

Possible consequences:

(1) You may find place to live.
(2) You may find an unadvertised place.
(3) You can ask landlords if they can suggest other landlords for you to call.
(4) It wouldn't cost anything.

147. STAY IN YM/YWCA, MOTEL, OR HOTEL

Possible consequences:

(1) You would have place to stay.
(2) It would cost something.
(3) You might still have to find a more permanent living situation.

148. MAKE REPAIRS, AND ASK
      LANDLORD TO PAY

Possible consequences:

(1) Poor housing conditions would be repaired.
(2) You will make it a more pleasant place to live.
(3) You will have to do the repair work yourself or make arrangements to have them done.
(4) You may not have to pay for repairs.
(5) Landlord may become angry and/or refuse to pay.

149. MAKE REPAIRS, AND PAY FOR
      THEM YOURSELF

Possible consequences:

(1) Poor housing conditions would be repaired.
(2) It will make it a more pleasant place to live.
(3) You will have to do repair work yourself or make arrangements to have it done.
(4) You will have to bear the expenses for the repairs.

150. CALL CITY HOUSING INSPECTOR

Possible consequences:

(1) They may be able to require the landlord to make the desired repairs plus any others required by law.

(2) They can give you the names of people and agencies who may be able to help with housing problems.
(3) Talking to an inspector doesn't cost anything.
(4) They may be able to force landlord into paying fully for needed repairs.
(5) It may result in faster action than you talking to your landlord.
(6) It may make your landlord angry that he was forced to make the repairs.
(7) It may take time and many phone calls to get any action from City Hall.

151. TALK TO AREA REAL ESTATE AGENTS

Possible consequences:

(1) They may know of several places in which you might be interested.
(2) They will have you on file and will contact you when something in which you might be interested becomes available.
(3) You will have to pay realtor's fees if you buy something through them.
(4) You will have one real estate agent with whom you can continue working, regardless of how much time passes while you are looking for a house to buy.

152. BUY HOUSE FROM LANDLORD

Possible consequences:

(1) It would mean you would not have to move.
(2) You would have to arrange finances to make down payment and mortgage payments on the house.
(3) You would be your own landlord.

153. FIND A DIFFERENT PLACE TO
      STAY TEMPORARILY

Possible consequences:

(1) It would remove you from problems of living with that relative.
(2) You may have to move in with other relatives or friends, which may result in similar or different problems.

(3) It would only be temporary, so you would still be looking for a place to stay.

154. HAVE HOME MOVED

Possible consequences:

(1) You would no longer live in un-desirable location.
(2) You would be able to keep living in same home.
(3) It may be very expensive.

155. THREATEN PERSON INVOLVED

Possible consequences:

(1) It may motivate person to act better.
(2) If it works, it would decrease problems.
(3) It may cause bad feelings between you and the other person.
(4) If that person still doesn't act right, you may have to carry out threat or feel badly about yourself.
(5) You might get hurt.
(6) You may have difficulty explaining your actions and threats to other people.

156. ASK CHILD TO MOVE OUT

Possible consequences:

(1) It would stop problems created by the child's living in your home.
(2) It may create bad feelings between you and your child.
(3) You may lose contact with your child.
(4) It may create other new problems at home.
(5) It may lead to your having a bad reputation among friends and relatives.
(6) It may cause an investigation into your family affairs by people from juvenile court.

157. CALL THE LOCAL EQUAL EMPLOYMENT OPPORTUNITY OFFICE

Possible consequences:

(1) They can solve discrimination problem on job.

(2) It may create bad feelings between you and your employer or other employees.
(3) It is free.

158. TALK TO COSMETOLOGIST

Possible consequences:

(1) Cosmetologist may have useful suggestions about how to improve your appearance.
(2) A consultation to give you sugges-tions might be free.
(3) Making recommended changes may be costly.
(4) It may help you feel that you are doing something for yourself.

159. JOIN WEIGHT WATCHERS

Possible consequences:

(1) They may help you lose weight and keep it off.
(2) You will meet a new group of people, whom you might like.
(3) It will help you feel that you are doing something about your appearance and health.
(4) It will give you the comfort of being with people who understand your problem.

160. GET MORE EXERCISE

Possible consequences:

(1) It may help you lose weight and improve your muscle tone.
(2) You may enjoy the feelings gained from exercise.
(3) You may feel good about yourself for getting yourself into better shape.

161. MAKE YOURSELF DO WHATEVER IS NECESSARY IN HOPES OF SOLVING YOUR PROBLEM THAT WAY

Possible consequences:

(1) You may prove to yourself that you can overcome your own problem.
(2) It may be very anxiety-producing to you to have to do whatever you are having problems doing.
(3) It may not help you overcome your problem.

(4) You may find that with the practice of making yourself do whatever is necessary, your willpower and personal strength grow stronger.

162. CHANGE THE SITUATION

Possible consequences:

(1) It will mean you will be out of the situation in which you are having the difficulties.
(2) It may mean there will be few situations left in which to interact with people.
(3) It may not help you overcome your problem.
(4) It might make your problem worse.
(5) You may have to explain to people why you are changing your patterns and lifestyle.
(6) You might prove to yourself that you can overcome your own problems.
(7) You might feel disappointed with yourself for avoiding the difficult situations.

163. TRY DIFFERENT THINGS AND SEE WHICH YOU LIKE BEST

Possible consequences:

(1) You might discover something you really enjoy doing.
(2) You may have enjoyable time doing things while looking to develop a hobby.
(3) You may meet new people in the process.
(4) You may do things you have never tried before.
(5) You might find interests that take your mind off your problems.
(6) You might feel much more confident about yourself as you develop new skills of which you are proud.

164. GO TO HOBBY SHOP FOR IDEAS

Possible consequences:

(1) You might discover something you might really enjoy doing.
(2) Salesperson could give you ideas.
(3) You may see something in the store of which you would never have thought.

(4) Hobby shop may offer lessons in various creative skills.
(5) It will cost something.

165. LOOK IN THE YELLOW PAGES OF THE PHONE BOOK

Possible consequences:

(1) You will find specific number for which you are looking.
(2) It will have listings of all professionals in your geographic area plus their telephone numbers and office addresses.

166. COMPLAIN

Possible consequences:

(1) It may stop the problem.
(2) It may create bad feelings between you and the person to whom you complained.
(3) It may make you embarrassed.
(4) It could help you feel that you are trying to correct the situation that is bothering you.

167. MAKE APPOINTMENT AT COUNTY MENTAL HEALTH CLINIC

Possible consequences:

(1) You can obtain marital counseling.
(2) You may not know anything about your counselor before you have your first meeting.
(3) You may have to pay a fee, but it would be a lower fee than a private counselor would charge.
(4) You can find out what other services are available.

168. DESIGN YOUR OWN DIET OR FOLLOW A FORMAL DIET

Possible consequences:

(1) It may lead to your losing weight.
(2) You would not have expense of doctor's visit.
(3) You have no way of knowing how medically safe the diet is for you.
(4) It would help you feel that you are working on solving your weight problem.

169. JOIN YMCA/YWCA; JOIN CLUB OR GROUP

Possible consequences:

(1) It will make you feel better about yourself because you will be doing recreational and social activities.
(2) You will meet new people.
(3) You may try new activities that you might find you like.
(4) It may involve some expense.
(5) You may improve your weight and figure as well as your spirit and mental attitude.
(6) It may take your mind off some of your previous problems.

170. JOIN SOCIAL ACTIVITIES PROVIDED BY CHURCH OR SCHOOL

Possible consequences:

(1) You will meet new people.
(2) You may do new activities that you might like.
(3) It will make you feel better because you'll be doing something to try to improve your social life.
(4) It may involve some expense.
(5) You may feel uncomfortable going to social activities by yourself, and may not feel that you have anyone to go with.

171. FIND A SPEECH THERAPIST

Possible consequences:

(1) Therapist is specially trained to help people with speech difficulties.
(2) It may involve an expense.

172. CALL AREA CHAPTERS OF ALANON

Possible consequences:

(1) Alanon is an organization of people specially trained to help the family members of alcohol abusers.
(2) Your request for help is confidential.
(3) They may be able to give you good ideas about how to cope with your family situation.
(4) It will give you the comfort of talking with people who understand your situation completely.

173. CALL LOCAL CRISIS HOT-LINE

Possible consequences:

(1) Most hot-lines are open twenty-four hours a day, seven days a week.
(2) It may help you just to have a friendly, understanding person with whom to talk.
(3) Most hot-lines have extensive information on every office, agency, and helping resource in the area, so they can help you contact whomever you need to.
(4) Your conversation will be confidential.
(5) They may be able to offer you immediate direct assistance.

174. HELP CHILD ESTABLISH NEW ACTIVITIES AND HOBBIES

Possible consequences:

(1) Child may be reassured when your efforts to help are obvious.
(2) Child might develop a more positive attitude about life in general when new activities are found that are fun.
(3) Child may gain self-confidence as new skills are obtained.

175. BECOME A VOLUNTEER IN A COMMUNITY SERVICE AGENCY

Possible consequences:

(1) Your self-respect and self-confidence will increase when you see that people in your community need your services.
(2) Finding new friends will be easier.
(3) Your own problems may not hurt you so much when you become more familiar with other people's problems.
(4) You need to arrange some kind of transportation.
(5) Volunteers receive no pay (or only very small stipends).

176. CONTACT CREDITORS TO ARRANGE PARTIAL PAYMENTS

Possible consequences:

(1) Your creditor will see that you are really trying to pay your bills.
(2) Creditor may help you make arrangements for reduced payments.
(3) Reduced payments would ease your financial problems.
(4) Creditor might not cooperate at all.